FREE THE PIZZA!

A SIMPLE SYSTEM FOR MAKING GREAT PIZZA WHENEVER YOU WANT WITH THE OVEN YOU ALREADY HAVE

BLAINE PARKER

Free The Pizza: A Simple System For Making Great Pizza Whenever You Want With The Oven You Already Have by Blaine Parker

Published by Slow Burn Marketing LLC, PO Box 982521, Park City UT 84098

For permissions, contact:

bp@slowburnmarketing.com

ISBN 979-8-9862051-1-3 Ebook

ISBN 979-8-9862051-0-6 Paperback

ISBN 979-8-9862051-2-0 Hardcover

CONTENTS

THE CHEAT SHEETS

DO YOU WANT TO MAKE GREAT PIZZA AT HOME?

If so, welcome. *Free The Pizza* represents a very narrow slice of the broad and complex world of pizza culture.

There are plenty of long, exhaustive books on this subject. This is not one of them.

The main focus here is the tools and techniques required for you to make an excellent, crowd-pleasing, American-style pizza on a regular basis. It will make everyone you know happy.

Free the pizza!

THREE ARTICLES OF FAITH FOR THE HOME PIZZAMAKER

1. This is not a throwdown. Pizza is love and joy for all.

2. You get out what you put in. Effort and ingredients matter.

3. Don't rush. Great pizza is patience.

WARNING

I am not a professional chef. I don't know what I'm talking about.

There are some professionals and self-declared experts out there who will tell you that what I am about to put forth in this modest volume is heresy.

They may be right.

I am not a chef, nor have I made pizza professionally. But as of this writing in 2022, I've been making pizza successfully since 2003.

I've made more pizzas than most people have eaten in their lives.

Sometimes, I am making pizza every night of the week. I have made pizza in ovens across the country for unsuspecting victims who declare it the best pizza they've ever had.

But they probably don't know what they're talking about, either.

FOREWORD

What an adventure in pizza. How did we get here?

My wife, Paige and I were in the middle stages of opening a new butcher shop concept in Park City, Utah. I was busy wearing the hats of managing partner, chef and butcher, along with many other toques as one does these days in food and beverage. While this was all going on, we were asked to sit down with Blaine Parker and his wife, Honey. They'd be interviewing us for their podcast about married couples running businesses together.

It was a wonderful afternoon. I mean, who doesn't love eating good food and talking about themselves?

The conversation revolved around me and Paige, husband and wife, opening a small business during a pandemic. If you lived through the joys of COVID-19, you might remember it was a time when none of us were having many guests. So I was eager to make lunch, sit outside and enjoy some company.

As promised, Honey and Blaine showed up with microphones and wine. In this case, they were kind enough to bring an underappreciated Italian red that's not well known in the state of Utah. (If we're lucky, it'll stay that way. More for us!)

Besides a platter of craft charcuterie, I was showcasing a 60-day dry-aged beef from the program we were developing for our shop. The conversation was engaging, and went longer than any of us expected. It felt like old friends had come by the house for lunch. Repeatedly, the conversation turned from business to food. And the one topic that seemed more vigorous than any other was: Pizza!

My program for the butcher shop includes hot sandwiches and other lunch dishes from a wood-fired oven, along with some pizza-related menu items. So we decided to have a kind of pizza exchange night at the house. I'd make some of the Alsatian flatbread and Detroit-style pizza I was planning for the shop. Blaine had his own plan to share a couple of creative sets.

In my life as a professional chef, I've worked in kitchens around the world and had wood-fired ovens to cook with. High heat and hardwood smoke are powerful companions. But this night, we were using just a home oven and we were baking on steel.

Blaine showed up and revealed his, um, "toppings." Wow. I admit I'm not a purist. There have been times when I've had, yes, the unspeakable Hawaiian pizza. (There, I spoke it.) But Blaine had other ideas. And when he said he was bringing a garlic and shrimp pizza with cilantro to the table, well... let's just say I've seen such things go so wrong the cat wouldn't even eat them. I was not hopeful.

When the bubbly garlicky shrimp pizza came out of our oven, he topped it with fresh plucked leaves of cilantro. I know that we had other great pies that night. But after one bite of this shrimp-sanity, the rest of the pizza that night was blocked out. It was a brilliant orgy of loving sensations on my tongue. The chew on the crust, the garlicky crustaceans, a pop of coriander. My wife even yelled out, "You don't want to open a pizza spot? WHY!"

As Blaine has said of *Free The Pizza*, it is not a cookbook. What it is, is a wonderful approach to and about pizza. As you'll see in these pages, the pizza geek author comes at you with knowledge, candor, cunning and wit. Even if it's not a cookbook, the few recipes it does contain will take you to another place as it did for me and my family. It's a fun adventure as much for the home cook as it is for this professional.

Free the pizza! Even if that means topping it with cilantro and shrimp...

John Courtney
Chef, Owner/Partner
Chop Shop Park City
www.ChopShopParkCity.com

THE PIZZA STARTS NOW!

WHAT ABOUT YOU?

Will you be doing the three smart things that should happen next, including …

1. Reading this entire book before attempting pizza?

The book is short. Pizza is forever.

2. Using your hands instead of an electric mixer?

It matters. Really.

3. Printing the Cheat Sheets linked at the end of each of the relevant chapters?

They save time, money and remorse.

Will you ignore these things at your peril?

Truthful tale. Michael, an aspiring pizza mystic, once said, "I don't need all that." He forsook the book. He ignored all of the above and pursued instant gratification. His pizza fail was so epic, his dog ran away and his wife left.

Michael returned to The Way. He found the path to astonishing pizza. He now has wildly popular pizza parties every night. They dance on the table and try to not spill their wine.

His wife did not return. His dog prefers to live with the neighbor. But Michael doesn't care. His now ex-wife was a shrewish halfwit, and the dog stank of swamp gas and deviled eggs. Michael's home now smells of toasted semolina and happiness.

Free The Pizza!

PREFACE

FROM PIZZA FAIL TO "YOU'RE THE GUY!"

My wife and I do a show where we interview married couples in business together. Not long ago, we were talking to one couple where the husband is an award-winning professional chef. John and his wife, Paige (who is a sommelier of some distinction as well as a fine front-of-house manager) run a high-end butcher shop together. We were talking about the state of restaurant dining where we both live and agreed that it suffers from resort-town challenges. Among the great first-world disappointments is that there's no good pizza here.

Out of the blue, my wife says to this professional chef, "You know, the best pizza in town is in my kitchen." The chef looked at me and said, "You're the guy? I've heard about you."

Uh-oh.

This is a dubious distinction.

You never really want to have a reputation as an expert of something because then someone will want to push you off a pedestal you weren't looking for in the first place.

But the truth is I used to be a pathetic loser in the pizza department.

I really liked the idea of making good pizza at home. Something that was as good as the pizzas of my childhood memories.

Finally, through a series of lucky accidents, I started studying the history of pizza, different methods of pizza making, different kinds of American pizza, and it wasn't long before—voila!—I was making really good pizza.

The problem is simple: Most people have no frame of reference for what it means to bake a pizza. It's part chemistry, part biology, part thermodynamics and part fearlessness.

But, to make a good pizza, you have to also understand what makes pizza good. And in the instant-gratification, info-saturation culture, the desire to understand is scarce. The greater desire is to just do it. Want to make a pizza? Go online. Get a recipe. Follow the directions.

And fail.

Before you even begin to make a pizza, read this whole book.

It's not very long. It covers some important basics. And by the end of it, when you trot out your first pizza, you should find yourself mildly amazed at what you've accomplished.

And it's not far from that first pizza to, "Hey, I've heard about you!"

People love pizza.

Free The Pizza is about sharing the love.

GREAT NEWS

YOU ALREADY OWN A PIZZA OVEN

"$900 for a dedicated pizza oven? That's a lot of money for a one-trick pony. You don't need it."

This was my response to a friend who has been dabbling in pizza. This friend desperately wants a pizza oven. The electric oven under consideration was good for really only one thing: making pizza. It can't do much else. The friend clearly did not need it.

I'm saying this as a guy who's been making pizza since 2003, using everything from a 1950s vintage Wedgewood stove to a $2,000 wood-fired dome oven that lived in my kitchen for almost a decade. I also have a pellet-fired outdoor pizza oven; I've used cast-iron skillets and the ovens of friends from Wyoming to Mississippi.

It's not about the oven.

Yes, having a wood oven was fun. It also weighed half a literal ton. Metaphorically, it weighed even more.

The fun part was the aura. It seemed like magic. It was captivating for guests. People would just walk into the room when the oven was cold and dark and be in awe.

When it was fired up, and the slow, curling, orange flames were licking the top of the dome? It was mesmerizing.

It also took three hours of fire tending to get it to temperature. (It didn't help that we were living at 8,000 feet elevation.) That oven was a lot of work. I'm glad to be free of it.

Right now, it seems like small, outdoor pizza ovens are a growth industry. They're everywhere. There are some guys from Finland living in Scotland building compact pizza ovens for the United States so enchanted Americans can make traditional, Italian-style pizza in the Neapolitan tradition.

Has there ever been so much potential for an international incident?

There are social media groups dedicated to discussions about using such ovens. People go in there wearing their virtual chef hats and rail at each other about the right and wrong types of flour and the mortal sin of pineapple on pizza and how stupid you are for being unable to read the manual for your oven.

Relax, friends. It's just pizza.

And like I said, I have one of those small, outdoor ovens. I've used it to make some truly awful pizza.

But on any given day, I'm making some of the best pizza ever. It's coming out of an old, beat-up General Electric home oven.

That's because it's not about the oven.

Pizza doesn't come from an oven.

Pizza comes from the heart.

Yes, you also need your head. It requires a modicum of skills. But they're simple skills. Learn them, and you can make great pizza using just your home oven and a few simple tools.

Great pizza at home is not about buying expensive ovens and other high-priced equipment. It's not about fancy, $100 Italian peels and $600 outdoor ovens that you can use only in nice weather.

Great pizza at home is about being subversive and taking back the simple human power of baking.

Making pizza at home is about understanding what pizza is, why it wins friends and influences people, and why it brings joy to almost everyone except the crustiest knuckleheads who couldn't find joy if it was stuffed inside their chef hats.

I've sometimes called this practice subversive pizza. If being subversive sounds sinister, that's because subversives have subverted the power of the word. We're not talking about throwing Molotov cocktails. We're talking about slinging discs of joy.

Subversion is about taking power. Being a pizza subversive is about liberating the joy of pizza from the shackles of commercialization and bringing it home for your friends and family.

Truly great pizza is perceived as something that can come only from a commercial kitchen with institutional-grade equipment and professionals who've been schooled in the dark magic of dough and stuff.

Consider this: Pizza as we know it was born hundreds of years ago in the lowest of low-tech times and was often made by people who could not have read a book like this or any other.

Technology, institutions and specialization have separated us from some very simple skills. This book is a guide for taking back the power of the pizza.

You can do this.

You can wow your friends. You can delight your family. You can take your act on the road and do The Pizza Pie Dog & Pony Show at friends' houses. (I have a canvas bag for my steel, and another for my peels, trays and cutting board. The ingredients all go into a cooler. It's pretty efficient.)

Pizza is simple. Pizza is joy. People love pizza. Simplicity, love and joy do not come from an expensive oven. They come from the heart and you have the power.

Welcome to the land of the pizza subversive. You've been warned. Proceed with joy.

Free the pizza!

WHAT THIS BOOK IS

AND WHY YOU MIGHT RUN SCREAMING INTO THE NIGHT

This is not a cookbook.

There. I said it.

A cookbook typically contains step-by-step recipes for how to make a vast array of dishes. That is not this. Yes, there are a few recipes inside this slim volume. But there is more.

This book is a guide. It's a rumination. It has stories.

But at the end of it all, this book is power.

Not a lot of power. You will not be able to run the United States government by following the steps within this book. (Though, especially in light of how things have been going in both major parties, that assertion might get an argument.)

The power you obtain from this book will let you do a thing that makes people say, "This is the best pizza I've ever had."

Not everyone will say that.

But enough will say it that you'll know you're onto something. And maybe more important is that you'll get to say, "This is the best pizza I've ever made."

This book is a simple system for making great pizza at home.

"BUT I DON'T WANT A SYSTEM. I JUST WANT A PIZZA."

Then pick up the phone and order one. You can do it. Other people have pizza systems, too. Big, commercial ones.

To that end, I know someone with a second-degree black belt in the high-kicking Korean martial art, Taekwondo. He said he wanted to make pizza. I told him what book to read. The conversation went something like this…

"I don't want to read a book. I don't have the patience for that. I just want to wing it and make a pizza."

"Let me ask you a question. What would happen if I walked into a dojo and said, 'I know that Taekwondo requires developing the skills for force, power, speed, mass and breath control. But I don't have the patience for that. I just want you to show me how to break a board.'"

He laughed. "I just want some tips about cheese and sauce."

"OK. Get regular, whole-milk, low-moisture mozzarella, the brick, not pre-shredded, and any brand-name pre-made pizza sauce in the supermarket."

He made pizza.

The best thing we can say about it is that it was mostly round.

Do not be the black belt. Be the pizzamaker. It's more fun than breaking boards.

IS THIS YOUR EXPERIENCE WITH PIZZA?

You get a hankering to try making pizza. You go to the interpizzaweb and find a recipe. You follow the directions, more or less. You make some substitutions because those are the ingredients you happen to have on hand. You ignore some of the "best by" dates on the packages. You make something that looks vaguely like a pizza and tastes like nothing you want to eat ever again.

I've been there. It is a disheartening waste of time and ingredients.

Here are just a few of the technical challenges that occur with that slapdash approach:

- The wrong flour
- Expired flour
- Expired yeast
- Working too quickly
- Not enough water in the dough
- Too much yeast at elevation
- Using a pizza pan

- Using the dreaded rolling pin
- No peel

But really, here's the overriding issue with that pizzaweb approach: It does nothing to help the aspiring pizzamaker understand what makes pizza work.

Did you know that old flour can make it impossible to make a pizza? One of my worst pizza experiences ever was promising my 12-year-old niece I'd make her some pizza.

When I went to stretch the dough, it had no stretch. I was just tearing holes in it. I had no idea the flour I was using was about a year past its best-by date. The glutens couldn't develop and it was just a pile of paste.

I made pizza on some flour tortillas.

One of the worst things you can do in an effort to make pizza is work too quickly. My advice to anyone starting out making pizza:

DO NOT try to make pizza the same day you make the dough.

I recommend making the dough at least two days ahead. It's easier to work and it tastes better. A same-day pizza ends up with a characterless crust and nobody wants more.

When I moved from sea level to 8,000 feet elevation, my pizza was inflating like party balloons. A little research revealed that high-altitude bread baking requires a reduction in yeast.

Can't stretch the dough? Can't make it round? Is it breaking? There might be too little water in the dough. But how would you know that if nobody was explaining the nuances?

If the dough isn't stretching, maybe you resort to using a rolling pin. This results in a pizza that's not quite round. More like an amoeba. The crust is also dense, with no air in it and doesn't taste very good. A pox on the rolling pin!

THIS IS WHY A SYSTEM HELPS

The system eliminates guesswork. It removes the question marks. We're not just breaking boards. We're engaging in a process. Making a pizza is not the same as making the cookie recipe from the side of an oatmeal box.

Making a pizza is a series of nuanced tasks that come together to form a unified whole. In the coming pages, we're going to do the following as part of the system:

- A quick history of pizza as we know it
- Discussion of the kind of pizza we're going to make
- Showing you the simple tools for making pizza
- Making the dough
- Making the sauce
- Heating the oven
- Preparing the toppings
- Preparing the tools
- Assembling the pie
- Launching
- Baking
- Retrieving
- Eating

If this seems like a long list and you're daunted, don't be. We're going to talk about all of this in fewer than 20,000 words. We'll also show you photos of the process online at www.FreeThePizza.com. (If you're wondering why more photos aren't in this book, it's because we wanted to keep the price down. Pictures in books are expensive.) The photos we're going to show you are not professional images. They were taken in my kitchen using my three-year old Android phone.

This is all an effort to deglamorize and demystify anything and everything about doing this.

If you see how this goes in my ugly kitchen with my amateur photography, you can imagine how well it will go in your designer kitchen surrounded by your admiring and astounded friends and loved ones. (You will see some photos taken in designer kitchens. Rest assured, those kitchens belong to friends of ours. We like them. We don't live them.)

We're also not going to teach you to spin dough in the air. That is a recipe for disaster. It flings flour all over the place. It tears holes in your dough. It's unnecessary for anything but showboating for your astounded audience.

I've done it. I'm not an expert at it, but I can do it. Just be prepared to occasionally be scooping your dough up off the floor.

At the end of the day, this is about doing one thing: making any recollections of failed pizzas only a fond memory. By following a series of simple steps, you are going to be amazed at how much you learn to enjoy the thrill of making, serving and eating your own world's best pizza.

HERE NOW, THE WORLD HISTORY OF PIZZA IN THREE MINUTES...

There are all kinds of myths about how pizza happened. Most of what you know is probably wrong. That's because the person who told you what they know as historical fact is wrong. And that's all because, really, most people just don't know or care that much.

However, you and I care. The reason? Even a moderately accurate historical understanding of pizza informs the making of pizza. The link to tradition is surprisingly useful.

Now, about that word...

First, let's forget about trying to figure out what the word "pizza" actually means. Word geeks can't agree on the etymology. Some theories include the following:

- It's derived from the Greek word "pita," which is another kind of flat, round bread.
- It's related to the Italian word for "pinch," as in reaching in and pinching the edge to pluck it from a hot oven.

- It's linked to the Latin word for "pound" or "stamp" as in made flat.
- It's related to a Lombard word for "mouthful," which in turn is related to the English words "bit" and "bite," and is also vaguely related to a German word for "snack."

Pita. Pinch. Pound. Stamp. Bite. Snack. As with the never-ending argument over whether pineapple belongs on pizza, there is no scholarly concurrence on where the word "pizza" comes from.

Personally, I like the theory about it being related to "pizzico," the Italian word for "pinch." It's a verb! It's action! It's hands-on! It's a direct connection to the pizza and the making thereof. And yes, more than once, I've reached into a hot oven and pinched the crust with my fingers to spin the pizza or pull it out onto a pizza tray. (This is not a recommendation to try it. I've also burned myself doing it.) But most likely, the word "pizza" is related to the Greek pita.

The evolution of pizza...

There have been pizza-like foods for about 10,000 years, ever since man began farming at the end of the Stone Age. While we have progressed way beyond the Stone Age, our culture still thrives on pizza and pizza-like foods. The more things change, the more they continue to look like pizza.

Fast forward from Neolithic times to the Kingdom of Naples, Italy in the 1700s and 1800s. What we recognize as pizza is beginning to evolve. Standard toppings include garlic, salt, lard and cheese. Somewhere in there comes the tomato. Just as nobody can agree on the origins of the word "pizza," nobody can agree on who added tomatoes or when, only that they were a New World import. That said, it's easy to agree that tomatoes had to happen.

About this time, there emerges a legend of the pizza Margherita. The Margherita is considered the archetype for Neapolitan pizza. In 1889, after the Unification of Italy, Italy's Queen Margherita makes a visit to Naples. The royal palace commissions a pizzaiolo by the name of Raffaele Esposito to create a pizza in honor of the queen's visit. He makes three pizzas. The one she likes best is the one that represents the green, white and red of the national flag of Italy. It is topped with tomato (red), basil leaves (green), and mozzarella cheese (white). Hence, the pizza is named in Queen Margherita's honor. While nobody can agree on the origin stories for the word "pizza" or the addition of tomatoes, there's broad concurrence that this story is a crock. Nonetheless, it continues as a fixture in pizza lore.

It's worth noting that Naples continues to take its pizza very seriously. There's even an organization called *Associazione Verace Pizza Napoletana*. That translates as "True Neapolitan Pizza Association." The AVPN is like the Good Housekeeping Seal of Approval for pizzerias who make their pizzas in the proper tradition of the Neapolitan pizza masters. The rules are strict, but pretty simple. Pizza may be baked in wood-fired ovens only. The dough may contain only 00 Italian flour, sea salt, fresh yeast and water. The cheese is water-buffalo mozzarella from the marshlands of Campania and Lazio. The tomatoes are San Marzano plum tomatoes from the volcanic plains south of Mount Vesuvius.

Is it significant that, as of this writing, the iconic chain, California Pizza Kitchen, has stores in Australia, Guam, India, Hong Kong, Japan, Mexico, the Philippines, Singapore, South Korea and United Arab Emirates, but none in Europe? Would anyone like to see CPK troll Naples by saying they're going to open a store there? "Yes, we believe that Naples is ripe for something different in pizza. People are getting tired of all Margherita all the time. Thai chicken pizza! That's the ticket!"

As you might imagine, pizza in Naples is distinctive. It's very soft and has a unique look and flavor. Speaking as a pizza geek, I believe in honoring Neapolitan pizza for all kinds of reasons.

I also do not enjoy Neapolitan pizza as much as American pizza.

I say this having had some excellent Neapolitan-style pizza in Los Angeles, Seattle, Salt Lake City, New York and (yes) Naples. But, I still prefer the American evolution of the Naples tradition. As we continue through this dance called pizza making, we'll be calling on some Neapolitan tradition while bringing the subversive twist of American pizza.

Anyway, in the late 1800s, pizza is brought to the United States with Italian immigrants. The keystone of the American pizza tradition is established in 1905 with Lombardi's on Spring Street in New York. One of my personal top favorites if for no other reason than its legacy, Lombardi's is the oldest licensed pizzeria in the nation. Let's call it the birthplace of American pizza, because we can. Feel free to argue it.

After World War II, the popularity of pizza in the US increases rapidly. Returning GIs who'd been to Italy have met pizza and have approved. Call it one of the benefits of creeping globalization. However, the evolution of pizza in this country leads from neighborhood pizza joints to chain pizzerias, frozen pizza, pizza-making robots, and all kinds of unfortunate creations masquerading as pizza.

And really, there is very little about pizza that is complicated. While following a strict AVPN code of pizza conduct is extreme, the home pizzamaker can take a cue from the iron fist of certified Neapolitan tradition. The power of the pizza is in purposeful and intentional preparation.

Understanding Naples pizza informs a better American pie.

THE KIND OF PIZZA WE'RE MAKING AT FREE THE PIZZA

When I started making pizza in 2003, my preferred style was the one known as neo-Neapolitan. That's an Americanized version of traditional Neapolitan (00 flour, water, salt and yeast), but made with higher-protein bread flour, along with olive oil and sugar. It has more structure than a traditional Neapolitan pizza, and is the precursor to what is now known as New York style pizza. It's the kind of pizza they make at Lombardi's, and at the famous Sally's and Frank Pepe's pizzerias in New Haven, Connecticut. That's the kind of pizza this pizza geek was making at home.

Then, in 2020, we were locked down. Hello, COVID!

In the early days of pandemic-inspired supply-chain issues, supermarket shelves were bare of bread flour. Even yeast was hard to find. So, I decided to take that as an opportunity to dabble some more in traditional Neapolitan pizza dough.

But I couldn't help myself.

Despite changing my dough recipe, I avoided making a soft, squishy Neapolitan pie. I kept going along with a more crusty, less squishy vision. While my preferred pizza dough is now a throwback to the old country, my pizza style is distinctly American.

The reason for bringing it to this book is simple: It's just easier. Besides pandemic shortages (which are over at the time of this writing—fingers crossed), I've also been into stores where you just can't find bread flour. Of all places, I was in Vermont around 2010, looking for bread flour in a series of small grocery stores, and couldn't find any. That's ironic because a) Vermont is a place with a high per-capita incidence of bread baking, and b) Vermont is home to noted flour giant, King Arthur Baking. Go figure.

Bottom line: this book is going to be talking about using a traditional old-world recipe to fashion a new-world pizza.

If you want to try making the old-world style pizza, you have that option. But we're not going to be pursuing it in this book. In the promise of offering a simple system, playing the Naples card clouds the issue and mixes a metaphor.

There are two specific differences between our pizza dough recipe and that of Naples. One is the use of store-bought yeast instead of fresh, home-grown yeast. Growing such a culture is a whole other book.

The other difference between our dough recipe and what they would make in Naples is that we are not specifying 00 flour. It's a finer grind than American all-purpose flour. It's also expensive and hard to find, so we're just not going to go there. If you ever ascend to a level of pizza geekdom that has you seeking out 00 flour, you'll be able to find links to various providers at the Free The Pizza website.

We're also not going to be talking a lot about traditional Neapolitan sauce made from San Marzano tomatoes. They can cost 500% more than regular domestic canned tomatoes. While I often use San Marzano tomatoes (and love them), I typically use a high-quality domestic canned product. Generally, I use whole tomatoes. They're reputed to be higher quality than tomatoes that have been diced or crushed. Sometimes, I just use the bottom-of-the-shelf store brand. Other times, I buy high-quality tomatoes like Muir Glen organic, or certain organic store brands. My recommendation is to use whatever you can justify, expense wise. It will never be bad. They're still tomatoes.

If you still want to venture to the land of San Marzano tomatoes, it's important to know that they've been called the "fake Rolex" of canned tomatoes. There are a lot of canned tomatoes labeled as San Marzano, but they don't carry the DOP designation from the Italian government. DOP stands for *Denominazione di Origine Protetta*. That translates to "Protected Designation of Origin." It's a strict system for identifying distinctive agricultural products and from a specific place, and which have significant properties determined by the local environment. A DOP designation signifies you're buying the real deal. In the case of San Marzano tomatoes, the DOP designation guarantees you're getting the right strain of tomato, grown in the right place in the correct manner, that they're harvested by hand when they are the right size, shape, and color, and they are peeled when they're packed.

Bottom line: Buy only an imported Italian product bearing the DOP designation. The reason this all matters is that the San Marzano is an heirloom plum tomato grown in volcanic soil in the shadow of Mount Vesuvius, and yes: You can taste the difference. It's an excellent tomato. You don't need to use it. But when you do use it, you can tell.

As for the cheese, this is a whole other can of worms. There are innumerable cheeses to be used for pizza. We are going to be focusing on two simple, easy-to-find cheeses that can easily be part of your system and yield a really good, American-style pizza: low-moisture mozzarella and pecorino Romano. (If Romano is hard to find, there's no reason you can't use Parmesan.) There are many other cheeses you can use. After you get your system down, feel free to experiment. But in the short term, stick with these tried-and-true ingredients. They'll make you happy and they're easy to find.

As with the flour, if you find yourself unable to source any ingredients locally, there are product listings online at Free The Pizza. You can also find further intel about the things I'm saying you don't need to use, like San Marzano tomatoes and 00 flour. That's because, if you're like me, you have a morbid curiosity about unnecessary, high-priced ingredients for cooking. (I can't explain it. Maybe it's a forbidden fruit thing. Whatever.)

THE TOOLS FOR MAKING PIZZA HAPPEN

I have a theory. One of the biggest reasons for home pizza failure-to-launch is the tools mentioned in the following chapters. Most people don't own them. They try to get along without them. And the end result makes them ask, "What was I thinking?"

And they never try again.

Can you make pizza without these things? Yes. Mainly.

But at least one of these items is absolutely necessary in some form. The others make it much easier, and that ease is what helps eliminate barriers to entry. A modest investment in these items diminishes the terror and speeds your journey towards the best pizza you've ever made.

We're going to look at the following tools to help get you prepared to sling a subversive pie:

- Baking surface
- Peel
- Pan

- Cutter
- Dust

Why each of these things separately? This is going to sound crazy, but as a kid, I was often told, "You don't need that X to do Y." It often involved something like a piece of sports equipment that everyone else had. And we're not talking the newest Air Jordan footwear. No. We're talking about simple things like a better hockey stick. And I found that when I finally upgraded to the better piece of gear, I performed better. That's not to say I think everyone should have the best of everything, especially if they're not serious about playing the game. But I've found that it's better to get good gear at the outset so you're not playing from such a disadvantage at the beginning. I've never played guitar, but I've heard musicians say that if you try to play a cheap, badly made guitar, it will put you off ever learning the instrument.

We don't want that to happen here. And pizza is easier than guitar and tastes better.

Anyway, the point here is that if you understand what makes a piece of equipment useful, it helps you make a better and more informed decision. You can go into this with your eyes open and aware of the limitations you're facing.

TOOLS: THE BAKING SURFACE

This is the one item that you can't do without. It's also the one item that I recommend being discriminating about. A robust product will make you happier. We're going to be baking with the highest heat possible from a home oven. Cheap and weak translates into dead and buried.

The key phrase here is "thermal mass." We're looking for a heavy, flat surface of dense material that doesn't conduct heat well. It takes a long time to heat up, and a long time to cool down. In the interim, it maintains a relatively stable temperature.

Time-honored baking surface materials include ceramic, stone and metal. Even though it's called a "stone," we're going to ignore the idea of anyone fabricating this item of actual stone. I've never seen a pizza stone made from an actual rock though I'm sure they're out there. And even though baking on a block of salt has become all the rage that seems impractical for our purpose. (Watch me change my tune in *Free The Pizza II: The Sodium Brick Baking Challenge*.)

We're going to look at the best baking surface, the runner-up baking surface, and the secret-weapon-on-a-budget surface. We'll also talk about some options that aren't the best. (Knowledge is your friend.)

BAKING STEEL

For my money, nothing beats the baking steel. This is a godsend for anyone who's serious about making killer pizza at home. At this writing, I've been making pizza for almost 20 years. Year one was the fabled hockey-stick curve. Bam! Went from making zero pizza to straight up near the top. Then, it leveled out. Since then, my pizza has been improving by small increments. Adding steel to my baking tools has been one of the biggest small changes, if that makes sense.

I like to make big pies, so my preferred steel is 16 inches (which doesn't fit in all ovens).

I also like to make a lot of pizzas, so I go for the thickest steel available, which retains more heat under ongoing use.

Do you need to start with steel? No way. It's expensive and it's heavy. But it's good to know that it's there. As you become serious about your baking and taking back the power of the pizza, you'll want steel in your sights. That said, if you want to take the plunge and start out using steel, go for it. Good tools can often accelerate the learning curve, speeding the acquisition of expertise.

BAKING STONE

The baking stone is probably the best known of baking surfaces. Sometimes, they're called pizza stones. That sounds like something you earn when you make a great pizza. "Hey, he got his pizza stones!" Not that anyone has ever said that until just this second. And we're going to try to make sure it doesn't happen again. But the stone is the most widely available product.

But beware. The stone can also be the most unreliable product.

If you've tried a stone in the past, one of the things you may have experienced is that a stone can crack. The phrase is "thermal shock." Too much heat too quickly and BLAMMO. This can sometimes be mitigated by properly "seasoning" the stone. (Maybe "curing" the stone is a better word. I've never heard anyone use it. But I like it.) Putting the stone into a cold oven, heating it up, then cooling it down can make it more resilient. This can possibly prevent later breakage under high-heat conditions.

That is, of course, if you're using a cheap stone. There's a more expensive stone out there that is more resistant to thermal shock. After breaking cheap stones, the product that I began using (before upgrading to steel) is a ceramic blend made from the same material you see in commercial deck ovens in pizzerias. This stone is thick, dense, robust, and while it does need to be "cured" or "seasoned" or whatever you want to call it, my experience is that it does not break. Spending more at the outset can save a lot of money down the road.

There are, of course, cheaper stones. They're usually beige, thin, and inspire little confidence. You can find them in your local kitchen stores, big-box retailers, and online for not a lot of money.

Warning: When using the baking methods espoused in this incendiary little book, a cheap stone will probably break.

TILES

There is an even cheaper alternative to the ceramic stone: tiles. Others have had great success with them. I have not. They break, too. But they're also very inexpensive, so replacing them isn't as daunting. We're talking about unglazed quarry tiles or terra cotta tiles from your local home improvement store. You buy several of them, group them on the oven rack to form a baking surface, cure them, and use them until they break, and then you replace them.

Let's be clear: I do not recommend this. The tiles are not designed for this. They're not necessarily safe for food. I mention it only because others talk about it as a hack. I've tried it and it didn't work out well. If the challenge here is to avoid basic frustration, this seems like a step backwards. My goal here is not to spend your money for you. This is about having a system that works and that you can feel good about. And I admit: There is something very, very satisfying about creating a killer product using cheap materials. Just as it's not about the oven, it's not about the stone. It's about what you produce with it.

THE LOW-BUDGET SECRET WEAPON

Yes, this is my secret-weapon baking surface. This is so unlikely, so seemingly obvious, and so not what the manufacturer had in mind. At least, I don't think it was. But what do I know? There is a category out there in cookware called the "pizza pan." It is useless for our needs here. They are flimsy round metal pans for making pizza-like objects that don't represent the transformative magic we're talking about here.

However…

There is a cast-iron "pizza pan" on the market. It costs slightly more than some lesser ceramic stones, and it is a sound alternative to both the stone and the steel. It performs better than the ceramic, and works almost as well as the steel for about half the price.

Product availability and manufacturing changes with the day, it seems. In the wake of all the quarantine cooking going on during the pandemic, this item became hard to obtain and the price kept going up. Because of this, I'm working to maintain a list of products on the *Free The Pizza* website. It is updated as we monitor prices and availability. There are also links to the products on Amazon. Of course, you can get your intel from the website and shop locally if you prefer. Either way, in order of preference for my money, this is how I'd rank the baking surface products:

1. Steel is the best, and is a good investment in your pizza future
2. Cast iron is the secret weapon and a good alternative to steel
3. Ceramic stone is the runner up, but the more expensive stones are preferable
4. Unglazed tile from the home improvement store is not something we recommend

You can see what the various options look like at the Pizza Tools page at *Free The Pizza*.

PEEL AWAY

The peel is that big, paddle-like item used to launch and retrieve a pizza. This is also the tool that nobody ever has on hand the day they suddenly say, "Hey, let's try to make pizza!" A lot of beginners go find a pizza recipe online, and it says something like, "Hey, if you don't have a peel, just use an upside down baking sheet!" I've tried that. It's no fun. It's unwieldy. That said, since developing the pizza habit, I've done some wack-job things. I've actually used a sheet of corrugated cardboard as a peel and lived to tell about it.

But I still recommend using an actual peel.

And if you're interested, the reason it's called a peel is because the word comes from the French word *pelle*, for shovel. Is it just me, or are there just not enough foods one can prepare with a shovel?

THE WOODEN PEEL

The wooden peel is (surprise!) made of wood. You've probably seen them being used in typical, American-style pizzerias, especially those that make "New York style." You can buy them in restaurant supply stores, sometimes in kitchen stores, and always online. (Again, you can find our recommended peels at the Free The Pizza website.)

You're going to find a lot of personal preference here, combined with budgetary decisions. When I was first starting out, I had only a wooden peel. I also bought one that's too big figuring, like buying clothes for a growing kid, it would be only a matter of time before I grew into it. And yes, I've graduated from 12-inch pizzas to 14-inch and even 16-inch pies. I've always been glad to have that bigger peel.

Here's another facet of the peel to consider: handle length.

If you're like me, and baking pizza in a home kitchen, you do not need a peel with a long handle. The handle on my 16-inch wooden peel is only 8 inches long. It is not only sufficient for working in a small kitchen, it's a really good idea. I have another peel with a 21-inch handle, and that can make things start looking like a slapstick routine. I've seen peels with handles that are nearly 5-feet long. In my mind, that conjures visions of swinging around with the peel and smacking bystanders in the head and then swinging the other way wiping out a shelf full of crystal stemware.

And yes, sometimes you have no choice on handle length. But if you're confronted with what seems like a very short handle, remember: The distance from your oven door to your baking surface is almost too short to measure. It's not like you're going to be raking around inside a gigantic commercial oven with seven pizzas going at once.

Another note on the wooden peel: It's great for launching the pizza into the oven. It's not as pleasing for retrieving, or for manipulating the pizza once it's inside the oven. I survived with wooden only for a long time before I finally broke down and bought a metal peel. Let's discuss that next, shall we?

THE METAL PEEL

Yes, the metal peel is kinda like a giant spatula. (Little bit of trivia if you're a word geek: "Spatula" comes from the Latin word, "spathula." It is informed by the Greek word "spathe," meaning "broad blade." Amazing or what?)

The blade on the metal peel is much thinner and easier for slipping underneath a pizza that's already in the oven. Once I've launched with a wooden peel, I rotate the pizza and retrieve the pizza from the oven using the metal peel.

Does this mean you need to do the same? No. You can make do with a metal peel or a wooden peel only. My own paradigm came from watching pizzaiolos in commercial American pizzerias and following suit. There's a reason for commonality in professional procedures. It works.

Some people swear by metal only. Some of those people sing the praises of their perforated metal peels, which are all the rage as I write this. I've never used one and don't plan to, at least not while I'm working exclusively with a home oven. It seems like a recipe for getting raw dough hung up on something on the way into the oven. If you want to see our picks for metal peels, you'll find them in the gear section at www.FreeThePizza.com

THE COOKIE SHEET VS. CORRUGATED CARDBOARD

Yes, lots of pros say you can use a cookie sheet in the absence of a peel. I've tried and I can't control it adequately. Maybe that's because I've never had one without raised edges, so I've always used them upside down. And as mentioned earlier, in a pinch, I've used a sheet of corrugated cardboard. That worked better for me. Of course, it had a very limited useful life. And I'm not recommending it. Don't try this at home.

Here's my position on the peel: it's not very expensive and saves a world of angst and a possible calzone moment. (That's when the pizza you're putting in the oven suddenly becomes an ugly pile of stuff and you try folding it into a calzone.) If you buy a peel and decide to give up pizza, it'll still look cool hanging on your kitchen wall. Get a peel and save your sanity.

CUT IT

Yes, we're going to talk about this. There are two basic tools available for this job. One is the wheel. The other is the blade. My personal preference: a robust, restaurant-style wheel cutter. It's easy to use, doesn't have much of a learning curve, and is easy to store.

The rocker-blade cutting knife known as a *mezzaluna* is big, more difficult to store, and takes some getting used to. It's the kind of thing that, when friends hear you make pizza, you receive as a thoughtful gift. (I own three *mezzalune* that I did not buy and have not used.) Try one if you wish. It's fun to watch a pizzaiolo who's skilled with this tool cut up a pizza. It gives you some flair. (I'm not seeking flair. I'm seeking pizza. Not to mention that it requires a whole other level of skill to slice a 16-inch pizza with a 12-inch mezzaluna, which is what you usually get from excited friends. There are longer ones. I've linked to some at our website.)

Here is the warning I offer about the pizza wheel: Don't get fancy. Big wheel, big handle, something robust you can whack into a pizza and feel good about. There are dozens of novelty pizza cutters out there. There's even one that looks like the Starship Enterprise, along with one that looks like a hatchet and another that looks like a circular saw. No doubt, every time you use it it's a laugh riot for your assembled friends. There's also an array of cutters that have no handle. You're just supposed grab it by the top of the unit and run it across the pizza. I've used one. I don't love it.

That's my recommendation. Your mileage may vary. I believe simple is best. Do what you want.

P.S. Before I had a wheel that made me happy, I just used a chef's knife. This isn't rocket science. It's not even pizza science. It's a pretty simple task.

You'll find the recommended pizza wheel at the Pizza Tools page at FreeThePizza.com.

THE SIMPLE SATISFACTION OF A PIZZA PAN

I went a long time without pizza serving pans (or trays, depending on your lexiconic preference). Once I had trays, I wondered why I waited so long. That said, you've probably only ever seen pizza pans in an American-style pizza joint. My experience with traditional Neapolitan pizza is that it's usually served on a plate. But that pizza is also only about 12 inches in diameter. When you're serving a 16-inch pizza on a communal table, a pan just makes sense. I've used a cutting board to serve pizza, which adds a nice, rustic quality to the presentation. But rarely does anyone have a cutting board big enough to serve a 16-inch pizza, or even a 14-inch pizza. (The biggest cutting board in my kitchen right now is 14.5 inches wide, which will just accommodate my average-size pie.)

Restaurant-grade aluminum pizza trays are relatively inexpensive, accommodate a pizza well (that is its job, after all), are easy to cut on, and make everything seem very together. At this writing, a 14-inch tray (my default-size pizza) sells for around 6 bucks. I've found that if we're having a pizza party, I need only two. I just keep them in rotation, cleaning up the used tray after serving the next pizza.

Take control with the aluminum tray. Or don't. It's up to you. Again, more info and links on the website.

DUSTING YOUR PEEL

OK, not really a tool. More like an ingredient. Here the word *dust* is doing double duty as both a noun and a verb. And probably nobody in the industry but me is using "dust" as a noun. The culinary elite talk about dusting their surfaces. Call me a rebel. But you're going to need to **dust** your peel with **dust** for sliding the pizza into the oven. Some folks just use flour. A favorite dusting substance is cornmeal. Personally, I prefer semolina. There are people who will tell you that "Cornmeal burns! Not semolina." Don't believe it. Semolina burns, too. There's black semolina all over my oven. But here's what's nice about semolina, which is a durum wheat product: Not only is it sometimes finer than cornmeal, it smells better in the oven.

It smells like the promise of better pizza to come.

There's nothing wrong with cornmeal. I recommend getting a more commercial and less artisanal product so the grains are more uniform. Some cornmeals are coarse and don't offer the same "ball bearing effect" provided by the smaller, finer, rounder grains in brands that your mother probably keeps in her cupboard.

Now, in a pinch, use what you have handy. I've been places where I've forgotten my semolina and the host has no cornmeal but there's a bag of polenta handy. And ya know what? Cornmeal and polenta are almost exactly the same product. But if you use a fine grind cornmeal to make polenta, it's going to be pasty. The good news is we're not making polenta. Whee!

DOUGH
THE FOUNDATION OF ALL THAT IS PIZZA

Without the dough, we have nothing.

Literally, without the dough, there is no pizza. All we have is sauce and cheese and toppings. You'd have to put it in a bowl and hand it to your friends with some feeble explanation about the "keto pizza alternative" or "pizza as our paleolithic ancestors would have made it because they didn't have bread."

Without dough, we have slop.

Here's the other thing to remember about pizza dough: Making a good dough is, all by itself, a raging success.

If you can pass this test, you are on the way to becoming a pizza demigod. We won't call you a pizza god because a) there are people worthy of the title who are far, far better than you or I, and b) we don't want to offend the hyper-religious among us who will take that use of a small "g" god designation as a reason to slam this book and leave a one-star review on Amazon. Though, maybe we should aim for that. Controversy sells.

Well, no.

The point here is not to be an antagonist. The point here is to be free from the shackles of commercial entrapment and bring the joy of pizza liberated into our own homes. But I digress. Whatever. Do this part well, and you're on your way to being a pizza demigod.

Back to the success of a good dough. Dough is not the easy part until it is. Understand, after almost 20 years of doing this, I'm still experimenting with pizza dough.

As I write this chapter, my second batch of "wild yeast" dough is fermenting in the fridge. In case you're wondering, "wild yeast" is a more literal description of what is widely known in the US as "sourdough." But the word "sourdough" is really just a description of the smell that comes from a particular strain of wild yeast bread dough made famous in San Francisco about the time of the California Gold Rush or thereabouts. French bakers brought their craft west from the old country, landed in California, and the rest is history. (As far as we know, during the Gold Rush, they did nothing about making pizza.)

USE YOUR HANDS, NOT A MACHINE

You may well have a stand mixer.

Don't use it.

I say this as someone who used a stand mixer for years. My pizza is far better now that I'm making dough by hand. And I admit, at first, that was not on purpose. When we moved into a condo we'd been renting out as a vacation property, my stand mixer was in storage. Without a mixer, I defaulted to the antique method of mixing dough. *A mano*, as the Italians would say. (*Fatto a mano* might be even more appropriate, since we're talking about pizza "made by hand," and every American in the room as juvenile as I am is giggling and saying, "He said fatto!")

Working the dough by hand, what I discovered was surprising: I was suddenly making better dough.

I'm convinced there are three reasons for this.

1. **The chance of over-kneading the dough by hand is virtually zero.** But use an electric mixer, and over-kneading is more likely to happen. Over-kneaded dough makes a tough pizza.

2. **You can actually feel the dough.** I've found that when I was living in a high-altitude, mountain climate, the weather impacts the making of dough with such regularity that it's never twice the same series of measurements and timing. With hands on the dough, it's easier to feel what's happening and what might need to happen. My dough is now better hydrated because I can feel the stickiness of the dough ball as it's being made. And it yields a better crust because it hasn't been kneaded into oblivion.

3. **I'm much more patient with it.** I also look forward to it. Making dough used to be an annoyance on the way to the joy of pizza. Like everyone else, I wanted my dough "fast!" Now, I look forward to it as a meditative part of the process. If you need it fast, buy it premade. Or, do what I do and take the dough out of the stock you made and keep in your freezer.

I'm also going to free you from the hardcore baker's belief that you need to weigh your ingredients. Yes, I did this for years. There's nothing wrong with it. I also found that, as mentioned previously with the climate, the measurements were largely irrelevant. And since my scales were in storage with my stand mixer, I needed to use measuring cups and spoons. I'd been thinking about getting my scales out. And there are benefits to having a scale handy. But I was watching one of those reality TV shows on basic cable where they go into different restaurants and interview the owner/chefs about their mad skills in making rustic food for the hoi polloi. One guy was making pizza dough, dumping a 40-pound bag of flour into a giant institutional mixer. When grilled by the host on how he wasn't weighing his ingredients, the man said: "Been doing this 23 years. Never weighed my ingredients." "Never?" asked the host. "Never," retorted the old man.

If not weighing pizza dough ingredients is good enough for a noted pizzamaker who's on national TV, it's good enough for me. But again, this requires you be in touch with the dough. You can't just dump in the quantity, knead it and walk away. You have to feel it and enjoy it and understand what you've got going on here.

Someone more Zen than I might say, "You need to be one with the dough." And based on the contents of this book, I'm clearly not very Zen. More like edgy, lapsed Episcopalian. And you know what?

You need to be one with the dough.

Make Your Dough For Tomorrow, Not For Today

This is one of the hardest things for the impatient pizzamaker: waiting to make pizza. And rarely do you see a pizza recipe that tells you that this is how you should be doing it. In the immediate-gratification culture, we all want to make dough now for pizza in an hour.

That doesn't work.

Yes, you can make a pizza-like object. Our goal is to avoid the PLO (Pizza-Like Object) in favor of something that wins friends and influences people.

And part of how that happens is by giving the dough time to sit in the refrigerator and get all cheery and glad to be alive.

Yes, alive.

Make no mistake about it: Your pizza dough is a living thing. Yeast are basically tiny fungi. Those little mushroom-esque creatures multiply inside the flour and water and bring the dough to life as a colony of impending pizza-pleasure organisms. And the longer they have to work, the better the job they do.

Up to a point.

· · ·

I always try to make my dough two days ahead at least. Sometimes, I let it sit for three. This is a little like aging a wine. The flavors in the dough become more complex, and the texture becomes more pleasing, and your dough becomes part of the equation required for that whole demigod status we were talking about.

So try to make your dough at least one day ahead, preferably two.

Also, feel free to experiment.

Make a batch of dough. Make one pizza today. Make another tomorrow. Make a third one on day three. (Who's really going to complain about eating that much pizza?) I've experimented with leaving a dough in the fridge for six days. My recommendation: Don't do it. Too long, and it starts to break down, it's unworkable, and doesn't taste great.

Two days is a good time frame. And anything that doesn't get used in two days can go into a plastic bag or container, and the plastic bag or container can go into the freezer. Wait, let me check…

I just checked. Inside my freezer are five dough balls. Two different kinds of dough. In a matter of hours, one of those frozen dough balls can be thawed and delivered to the table as a piping hot, arrestingly aromatic pie of pizza golly gosh goodness.

I have never said "golly gosh goodness" before. That's the effect this thought has just had on my pizza-addled brain. It's like a drug. Maybe I need to go thaw a dough ball. Or have patience and wait for the results of my wild yeast experiment.

Anyway, I digress. This is not about my pizza cravings. It's about your indoctrination. To that end…

LET'S MAKE DOUGH!

Part of the reason pizza happens is because of how well we develop the proteins present in the flour. (Yes, that's the gluten. Free the gluten!)

The goal in making the dough is to develop the gluten enough that it's strong and elastic and can support a pizza. This is one reason to let the dough proof in the fridge for a couple of days. It helps in developing the glutens. It also ferments somewhat to develop the flavor as discussed previously.

Here now, we're going to look at a recipe for Neapolitan-style dough. The hardass pizza people will get all over me for calling this Neapolitan-style because it's being made with all-purpose (AP) American flour.

That is why it's called Neapolitan-STYLE.

As alluded to earlier in this book, a proper, VPN-approved Neapolitan dough has to be made with an Italian 00 flour, which costs as much as a new limb or a black-market internal organ. You don't need that for this. AP flour is close enough. We're also not baking in a 900-degree wood-fired oven with an officer from the AVPN breathing down our necks, so there will be no hell to pay.

Again, Neapolitan-STYLE. It will not be baked in the Neapolitan style. It is merely our canvas to do with as we wish.

So, are you ready? Get ready to *sporcarti le mani*. (That means "get your hands dirty." Everything sounds more romantic and more fun in Italian, does it not?)

WHAT YOU NEED

FIRST, THE TOOLS:

A BIG BOWL

Big enough for your head with room left over is smart

ANOTHER BIG BOWL

Yes, you can clean out the bowl above. Either way, as long as it's clean.

A MEASURING CUP OR TWO

You'll need at least one. I use at least two. And just as a side note, I've become addicted to two different OXO Good Grips products: Angled Measuring Cups for the water and Stainless Steel Measuring Cups (with magnetic snaps!) for the dry measure. The snaps are great. The steel cups don't rattle in the drawer.

MEASURING SPOONS

You'll need standard measure spoons. As with the measuring cups, I've graduated to the OXO measuring spoons, too. Besides the snaps (no rattling around and getting stuck on things), the narrow profile fits more easily into spice bottles and yeast packets. (It's amazing how little details like this can really start to become a fixation. Every time I open the drawer containing the spoons and cups, I marvel at how they stay organized. But I digress.)

PASTRY OR BASTING BRUSH

You're going to need to brush some olive oil near the end of this process.

BOWL SCRAPERS

These are not required, but they are useful. These can be just about the least expensive kitchen tool you'll ever buy. I resisted them for years. I finally bought two for 99 cents, and realized I was being an idiot for eschewing them. They are little plastic cards with a rounded edge so you can scrape dough out of a bowl. Insanely simple.

BENCH SCRAPER

Again, not required, but useful. Also another tool I resisted for years. Great for cutting off pieces of dough before forming them into balls, and (yes) scraping stuff up off the work surface.

Again, links to many of the above items are on the www.FreeThePizza.com website if you want to see them.

NEXT, THE INGREDIENTS:

ALL PURPOSE FLOUR

I like to use King Arthur Organic AP flour when possible, and their standard AP when the price on organic is too high. But any good AP flour will do as long as it's NOT past its best-by date. I cannot emphasize this enough. A stale flour will not develop gluten and you won't get a pizza. And that will suck. Check the best-by date on that bag of flour in your pantry and then go buy a new one because you're going to find out it was last best when Carter was president.

WATER

Someone is going to try to tell you all kinds of lies about water. "New York pizza is great because of the water!" That's nonsense. There are lots of reasons SOME New York pizza is great, but the water is not the be all and end all. (Although, New York water is pretty good. Philly and Boston, too.) If the water is drinkable and doesn't taste ugly, you're fine. In a pinch, if your tap water is nasty, either get a filter pitcher like a Brita Stream, or buy bottled drinking water. (Not distilled. You want the minerals.)

TABLE SALT

Any table salt will do. I don't use kosher salt for this purely because of the measuring angle. (Kosher salt grains are bigger and measure differently.) There are distinct benefits to kosher salt in some cooking, like candy making. There's little difference in the chemistry for baking. I do use something that's crazy expensive (for salt) because you actually can taste the difference between it and regular salt. (If you care, it's an "ancient sea salt" product from Utah called Real Salt. I used to buy it in the supermarket in Utah for about 700% of the price of regular table salt. Since I've moved away, I buy it at Amazon for slightly more. But seriously, you don't need it. Consider it only if you're one of those knuckleheads like me who starts to get too granular with things. "Granular." Ha! Get it?)

INSTANT YEAST

Also known by the names "Quick-Rise" (Fleischmann's) or "Rapid-Rise," (Red Star), this is the yeast that I began using when making pizza in earnest. It doesn't need to be activated the way active dry yeast does. You just measure it into your dough and go to work. I've used the Red Star and Fleischmann's products, as well as Saf Instant Yeast. The latter is available by the pound. That's a lot of yeast. (The other two, I buy in sleeves of three 1/4-ounce packets. The price can be about 400% higher per ounce, but it is also more convenient.) And please, for the love of pizza, do not buy anything called "pizza yeast." It's an instant yeast, but contains a disagreeable additive. Your crust will taste like your least favorite brand of frozen pizza.

OLIVE OIL

This is purely for brushing on the inside of the second bowl. (This recipe contains no oil and no sugar. Other recipes do. That's for another time.)

HIGH-ALTITUDE NOTE: The amount of yeast called for in the recipe to come is the normal amount for this recipe at sea level-ish. When I'm working at 7- to 8,000 feet elevation, which I've done a lot, I cut my yeast in half. Otherwise, my pizza crust inflates like a blimp over Italian airspace. If you live above 4,000 feet elevation, you might want to try half the yeast as well.

THE STUFF THAT GOES IN THE DOUGH

5 cups unbleached all-purpose flour

2 teaspoons of table salt

1 teaspoon instant yeast.

1 ¾ cups cool water

PUTTING THE STUFF TOGETHER

Wash your hands. Please. Or, as the Italians would say, *Lavati le mani. Per favore.*

1. Get the large bowl and mix the flour, salt and yeast.

You can use a big metal spoon. Sometimes I use a fork or a whisk. Most of the time, I just sift it all around with my fingers.

2. Add the water.

Pour the water into the flour and stir it around. Get in there with your hand. Mix it all until combined. Then, really get in there and knead. I hold the bowl with my right hand and knead with my left as if it were an exercise from a martial arts class. Get aggressive. Use those muscles. Yes, it will be sticky and gloppy. But as you mix and the water combines with the flour, the hydrating dough in the bowl will begin pulling the shaggy dough from your hand.

3. Keep kneading until the water and flour are like one.

This should take about five minutes. You'll end up with a coarse-looking ball that's sticky to the touch. Not sticky? Try adding a tablespoon of water and knead some more. Too sticky? Try adding a tablespoon of flour and knead some more. By the end of this phase of kneading, you want a ball that looks rough and feels tacky. (If you find this exercise boring, turn on the radio to a good talk station or put on an audiobook. Catch up on your current events and your reading.)

4. Let the dough rest for five minutes.

This resting period is letting the dry ingredients become further hydrated. In fact, while that's happening, why don't you have a beverage as well?

5. After five minutes of rest, get back in there with your hand.

Keep kneading for several minutes until the ball begins to appear smooth. At this point, if it's easier to remove the dough ball from the bowl and knead it on a flat surface, go nuts. If I do this, each move is pulling the side of the dough nearest me up and away, folding the dough over on itself, then turning it 90 degrees and repeat. In a perfect world, it will remain a little tacky. That means there's a high enough percentage of water to make a better pizza. Yes, tacky is harder to work with. But in the end, it's worth it. Do you now have a slightly tacky, smooth-ish ball? Good.

6. Let's try the windowpane test.

Tear off a chunk of the dough. Roll it into a ball and flatten it with your hands. Try stretching it until it's thin and translucent. You should be able to see light through it. If so, this is great. If it's not doing the windowpane, if it just tears, let the dough rest a bit longer. Then try it again. If you want to feel like you're doing something, knead it a little more. I've found that sometimes I just have to walk away and let the dough sit longer. And sometimes, it's close enough to a proper windowpane that I let it go. As the dough sits and proofs, the windowpane often solves itself.

NOTE: I will often do a knead/rest session of four cycles before I'm satisfied that I've got a windowpane that makes me happy. Don't get bummed out if it doesn't work the first time. You'll get there.

WHAT DOES A WINDOWPANE TEST LOOK LIKE?

It depends on who you are. Seems like everyone has their own take on it. Mine looks like this. One of the things I do when I stretch it into a membrane is I try poking it with a fingertip to see if it stretches without tearing. It's always very satisfying.

1. Grab a little ball of dough and try stretching it between your fingers

2. I like to push against the windowpane to see how elastic it really is

7. Get the second bowl.

Presumably, it's clean. Brush it with a light coating of olive oil.

8. Dust a clean work surface with flour.

Turn the dough out onto it. Flatten it a bit and it will get a little squarish. Then grabbing each of the "corners," fold them over each other, gathering the dough together into a ball. (See photos below.) With the gathered side down, put the dough ball into the new, oiled bowl. Cover with plastic wrap.

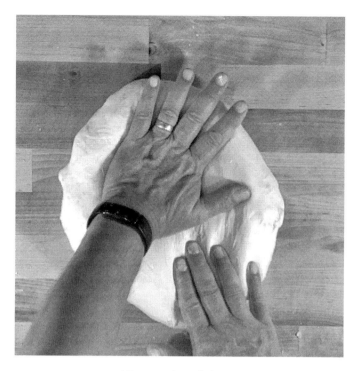

Flatten dough ball

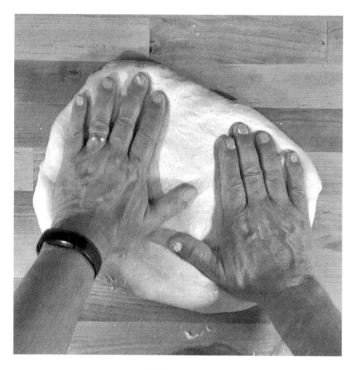

Flatten...

Fold one…

Fold two…

Fold three...

Fold four...

Grab and pinch folds together

Turn over and shape into a ball

9. After 20 minutes, repeat step #8.

Making sure there's a light dusting of flour on the board, turn the giant dough ball out onto the surface, flatten it again, fold over the four corners to make a new ball, and put it back in the bowl.

10. Repeat two more times.

Wait twenty minutes, flatten and fold again.

11. After the third interval, cover the bowl with plastic wrap again.

Let it sit on the counter for an hour or so. Then, move it into the refrigerator.

12. After 24 hours, bring the dough out of the fridge.

Turn the dough out of the bowl onto a lightly floured surface. Cut the dough into three, four or six balls. (I use either my chef's knife or a pastry scraper. The scraper is one of those things I resisted for ages, along with a bowl scraper. They cost very little, but are really useful.)

Three balls should yield three pizzas about 15-16 inches.

Four balls should yield four pizzas about 14-inches.

Six balls will yield six pizzas that are 10-12 inches.

(TIP: if this is your first time out, go with six balls. Smaller pizzas are easier to handle, at least psychologically. As you become more confident, you'll feel better about making larger pies. Even a 10-inch pizza feels like an accomplishment. When you get to 16 inches, you'll feel like a pro.)

STEP-BY-STEP PHOTOS OF SHAPING A PIZZA DOUGH BALL

Forming a dough ball from a giant batch of dough is a puzzling prospect. However, it's actually pretty simple.

The first thing you do after dividing the dough into pieces is grab a piece, flatten it and fold it over on itself.

Turn the dough 90 degrees, then flatten it and fold it over again.

Grab all of the "corners" that are now on one side of the dough ball, gather them all together and shape the dough into a ball.

Finally, pinch them all shut, twisting and pinching them again if necessary. (There is a video of this at the website, www.FreeThePizza.com/video

Flatten the piece of dough

Fold the dough over on itself

Rotate 90 degrees

Flatten and fold it over on itself again

Gather all of the corners together and shape into a ball

Pinch the bottom shut, twist and pinch again. You have a pizza dough ball.

13. Bag the dough balls.

Put each dough ball into a quart-size, zippered plastic bag. Brush the dough ball with a tiny bit of olive oil, and put all the dough back into the fridge.

IT IS ALIVE!

Congratulations. This is the part nobody ever tells you. Pizza dough is a living thing. No, it's not smart enough to do your taxes. It's not even sentient. But because of its aliveness, it can make *you* happy to be alive.

What next?

We wait at least 24 hours more. We're letting the dough get all giddy in there. After its time in the refrigerator, the dough balls should have increased in size.

Get ready to make pizza.

GETTING SAUCED

THE LOVE APPLE RULES

People always look at me a little bit sideways when I mention the love apple. I learned this as a little kid. Didn't anyone else? Centuries ago, when the Spanish brought the tomato to Europe from the New World, the French believed it to have aphrodisiacal powers. Hence, the tomato's nickname, *pomme d'amour* or "love apple." And if your pizza dough is the foundation, your tomato-based pizza sauce is the love party that is happening in your house called pizza.

Tomatoes are a gift to our taste buds from the deity of your choice. Yet, if you buy so-called "fresh" tomatoes in the supermarket, they're likely to be a hard, flavorless water-delivery system.

But if you can remember sometime in your life when you were handed a tomato straight from the garden, gave it a little salt and took a bite, you know how you were hit with that flavor explosion.

Speaking of love apples, let's also get past the silly argument that the tomato is a fruit and not a vegetable. It's not going to help us make better pizza, but it is going to give you some trivial ammunition when some joker thinks he's being funny by telling you he hates fruit on his pizza.

Remember the three basic taxonomy classifications of animal, mineral or vegetable? (Outdated, yes, but in ongoing use nonetheless.) You don't get a choice. Can you chew it without it running away? That means it's a) not a rock and b) not a chicken. As neither animal nor mineral, fruit is part of the vegetable kingdom.

Vegetables are the parts of plants that animals eat for food. (Ironically, they often contain minerals. How's that for a mind-bender?) Those vegetable parts can include flowers, fruits, stems, leaves, roots, and seeds.

Like the word "vegetable," the word "science" is very general. So let's narrow it down a little. Let's talk about botany. As you know, a botanist is a scientist committed to the study of plants. A botanist will tell you that a fruit is any class of vegetable that contains seeds.

So, let's see. If we walk into the vegetable section of the local Kroger, we can buy tomatoes, cucumbers, zucchini, and peppers—all of which contain seeds. If we make all these seed-containing products into a salad, why aren't we making a fruit salad?

Exit the botanist, enter the chef.

Speaking not from a position of science but from a position of the kitchen, these fruits are classified culinarily as vegetables.

So while the tomato is one of many fruits we find in the vegetable section, that is a scientific distinction and not a culinary distinction. If you're wearing a lab coat and a pocket protector, you know it's a fruit. If you're wearing an apron and a toque, you know it's a vegetable.

And at the end of the day, this distinction means nothing. But it does help you subvert any stupid arguments about taxonomy. (If you're a scientist, don't be emailing me about this. I already know it's a specious argument.)

The more important question is: Why on earth do we love the love apple so much?

When you bite into a tomato, both sugars and acids come into play. Those sugars and acids activate various taste receptors. At the same time, smell comes into the picture. Biting that tomato makes all kinds of volatile compounds float around and trigger receptors in your nose.

All this tasting and smelling action makes your brain happy.

Unless, of course, you bite into a common store-bought tomato that has the density of a softball and whose active compounds seem to be water and a color not red.

That's why we're not going to use fresh tomatoes from the supermarket. It's a crap shoot and costs too much money. This is an area where the canned tomato is your friend.

The quality of canned tomatoes also spans a spectrum. In my local supermarket, I can find a 28-ounce can of tomatoes priced anywhere from 99 cents to five bucks. It depends on various factors. The cheapest can on the shelf has a store-brand label. Who knows what it is and where it comes from? But it's whole tomatoes (which is good, as whole tomatoes are generally better quality tomatoes), and it can be used to make a pizza sauce by getting busy with other ingredients.

The can of tomatoes that costs five bucks has been discussed previously: the fabled San Marzano tomato grown in the volcanic soils with a picturesque view of the once deadly Mount Vesuvius. These tomatoes are amazing. You will like them. You do not need them. I love using them, but do so only on special occasions.

LATELY, THERE ARE TWO KINDS OF TOMATOES I USE AS A DEFAULT.

There's a store-brand organic tomato that's about two bucks for a 28-ounce can. And there's a store-brand of fire-roasted tomato that's available only in 14.5-ounce cans for about a buck. I've been using those a lot.

I also keep an eye out for sale prices on the name-brand organics and fire-roasted products and buy them in quantity when available. And I always have a couple of cans of San Marzano tomatoes in my pantry backstock. You never know when you might need them or just plain want them. (I also have to go to a local high-end supermarket or order them online. My regular supermarket no longer carries any tomatoes with the San Marzano name that also bear the official DOP stamp from the Italian government. If I'm going to spend five bucks on a can of tomatoes, I want the tomatoes I'm paying for. I've also tried so-called domestic San Marzano "style" tomatoes, and they're good—but they're not the same.)

My recommendation for this sauce: Use the best-quality tomatoes you can justify.

If you feel like this is an experiment and you want the bottom-shelf tomato, go for it. If you want to come screaming out of the gate with imported Italian product, go nuts. Either way, we're going to take those tomatoes and dress them up for freeing the pizza.

As mentioned, whole tomatoes are supposed to be better quality than diced or crushed. I can't prove that. I must take it on the authority of the culinary gurus. But know that if you use whole tomatoes, they're going to have to be made not whole. There are a couple of ways to do this.

If you have an immersion or stick blender, or you're willing to buy one, that's the easiest way to do it. I do that.

Sometimes, I just use a potato masher. It depends on the consistency I'm going for.

You can use a blender or food processor. Just make sure to do it while the tomatoes are cool. Invariably, you're going to put all this red soup into a blender, misapply the lid and have red splatter all over the joint. Proceed with caution.

If you want to crush the tomatoes the old-fashioned way, you can put your hands right into the tomatoes and squeeze them to pulpy bits. I sometimes do that with San Marzano tomatoes because it seems like part of the religious experience of using this sainted product.

If you use diced tomatoes and you want to get them smooth, it's still going to require some blending. Any of the methods above will be sufficient.

Ultimately, you want to end up with a coarse sauce that clearly contains tiny tomato bits.

Wait, what? Why am I not recommending pre-made pizza sauce?

For the same reason I'm not recommending pre-made pizza dough. We can use pre-made sauce, a pre-made dough in a tube, and heck—why not just buy the frozen pizza that puffs up when you bake it?

That's not freeing the pizza. That's keeping it tethered to greater commercial concerns.

We're talking about bringing pizza power into your own home kitchen. And making it all is what makes it all good. Just as nobody ever waxed poetic over a pasta dish made with canned sauce, nobody's eyes ever rolled back in their head with the joy of a partly-pre-packaged pizza anything.

All hail the homemade sauce!

Now, be prepared for this recipe. I measure nothing. You don't have to, either. I started working this way many years ago. People think I'm nuts. The reality is, you learn what's enough by eyeballing it. Understand, this doesn't work with baking. When you're baking, you're being a chemist. Quantities are important because of the chemical reactions that take place between elements like flour, water and yeast. When you're making a sauce like this, it's not predicated on any exact ratios of ingredients and how they behave. It's predicated on how it tastes and whether the consistency is right.

And if you think this approach to sauce is too cavalier, it might be worth noting: The earliest cookbooks often don't provide any measurements at all. There's a famous New Orleans cookbook that is a useful, metaphorical parallel for an American making a favorite food that's evolved from an Italian staple that relies on a vegetable that's classified as a fruit which was imported to Europe from South America. (Sounds like another international incident in the making.) It's an important cookbook called *La Cuisine Creole (Cooking In America)*. The author is

Lafcadio Hearn, a Japanese writer of Greek-Irish descent who spent time in New Orleans translating newspaper articles from French and Spanish into English. I own a copy of *La Cuisine Creole*, and the first time I saw it, I loved that the recipes say very little in terms of detail. No, Mr. Hearn offered no recipe for pizza sauce. But here's a recipe for Pigeon Pie:

PIGEON PIE. VERY NICE

Take six pigeons, truss them, and stuff them with their own livers, a little bacon, some butter, parsley, and rolled cracker or a small piece of bread; salt to taste; cover the bottom of the baking dish with slices of veal or beef; season with chopped parsley, mushrooms, pepper, salt, and butter. Place the pigeons on this, and cover with a nice pie crust. When the pigeons are placed in the pan, lay between each two pigeons the yolks of two hard-boiled eggs. Be sure and have enough gravy to keep the pie very moist. This can be done by adding plain beef-stock or water as the pie bakes. Parboil the pigeons a little, also the beef, before putting them in the pan, and then keep the water they were boiled in to fill up the pie.

Yes, this is the entire recipe. And really, the only thing preventing you from making this recipe is fear. Something about being provided with details regarding ingredient amounts, oven temperatures and step-by-step directions lulls us into a sense that everything's going to work out.

Back when I first began making pizza, I used to follow sauce recipes. And very quickly, I found myself in the realm of "adjust seasonings to taste." There was never enough of anything going on there. Enter stage right: pantsing.

You'll be getting much more detail about making pizza from this book than you would about making a pigeon pie from *La Cuisine Creole*. But we're still going to be winging it in certain areas. You'll be fine. You're going to get to fly by the seat of your pants where that's OK. You'll get details where details matter greatly. This sauce recipe is the first place where you get to pants it. Ready?

HERE NOW, THE SAUCE...

Use whatever tomatoes you desire. I recommend a mid-priced, higher-quality tomato. But it's up to you. Use the bottom shelf if you feel like this is just an experiment. Go right to the top if you're a hard-charging A-type who can't be bothered with anything but the best. (OK, who are we kidding? If you're a hard-charging A-type, you probably never made it this far. But who knows? Maybe you're a hard-charging A-minus. Either way, if you're that person and you made it this far, you are going to crush it in Pizzaville.) Personally, I'm a moderation-in-many-things type of guy. This is one of them. Middle shelf. So, here we go…

Ingredients

28-ounce can of tomatoes, whole, diced or crushed

Salt

Olive oil

Onion powder

Garlic powder

Dried basil

In this recipe, we measure nothing. Go with the taste. The key here is not the science of measurement. It's the art of "How does it dance on my tongue?" Does it taste bold and memorable in a good way?

Grab that 28-ounce can of tomatoes. Open it with a can opener. (Sorry this has to be said. There's reportedly a generational challenge with people of a certain age who don't own can openers and don't know how to use them.) Pour the tomatoes into a saucepan. Grind them up using an immersion blender or smash them with a potato masher. Turn the heat to medium.

While it's heating, add a healthy glug of good olive oil. Maybe about a tablespoon-ish. Maybe two.

Add salt to taste. You'll want the flavor of the tomatoes to begin waking up and make you think, "Hey, I'd eat more of that."

Add onion powder. If you were using a measuring spoon, maybe about a 1/2 teaspoon-ish. Garlic powder, add about half of that.

Add dried basil if you like. I use about a tablespoon-ish. It doesn't always pair with everything you're putting on a pizza. But for the beginning, especially this exercise, it's great.

When the tomatoes begin bubbling, reduce heat to simmer.

Let the pot simmer for long enough to reduce the consistency to a thick-ish sauce. It will be loose, but not watery. This can take 20-30 minutes or more, depending on how aggressive you are. I find that on a very low heat, 30 minutes is sufficient.

Again, taste it. Does it taste good? You're in!

If it doesn't taste salty enough, add salt. If it needs more herbal pop, add some more basil.

The sauce is ready when it's thick enough that it looks coarse and tastes good all by itself. If you taste it and you'd consider sitting down with the entire pot and a spoon, you've got pizza sauce.

P.S. ON COOKING THE TOMATOES

There is a faction out there that will take me to task for doing all this to the tomatoes, especially the sacred San Marzano. A lot of pizzamakers want you to put that tomato just about straight from the can onto the pizza unadorned. It has a marvelous flavor all by itself. I agree that it does. It is a very bright flavor that makes you oh so very happy. However…

Two things. One, I don't find the unadorned tomato has enough zip. Two, I don't want to cook with something that watery. Uncooked sauce has a high water content. It's very wet, and can make the pie sloppy in a home oven. Recently, I was using a friend's pizza oven and (for technical reasons we won't go into here), one of the pizzas came out soft and wet and somewhat like a traditional Neapolitan pizza. There was a lot right with it. But we're making a knockdown, drag-out pizza for the American palette. Wet and soft is not gonna fly. This pizza has to soar. Let us make it so.

THE CHEESIEST

This might be the most surprising part for a lot of pizza newbies: There is nothing fancy about the cheese.

Yes, it's possible to use fancy cheese. I've certainly done it.

But at the core of the most satisfying of the world's pizzas is the lowly low-moisture mozzarella. That's the white-ish cheese you buy in the one-pound block in your supermarket's dairy case.

There are all kinds of other, expensive mozzarellas. If you're making a VPN-approved pizza Margherita, you need to use DOP-approved, water-buffalo mozzarella imported from the Campania region of Italy.

We're not doing anything that fancy.

Remember, this is a system. A system is easily replicable. When you're done here and you get good at this, you will be confident enough in your pizza skills to make a pizza anywhere in the country with what you know to be available in your local supermarket, just as if you were gathering items for making a tuna melt.

WARNING!

Do not use pre-shredded cheese.

This is one of the several crimes against cheese. Pre-shredded or pre-grated cheeses have been treated. They are coated with an anti-coagulant. On a good day, it's potato starch. On a bad day, it's Natamycin, which is also known as pimaricin. Natamycin is used as an alternative to sorbic acid, which is an artificial preservative. So, not artificial? How bad can that be? Well, when it's not moonlighting on shredded cheese to preserve it and prevent it from clumping together, Natamycin is used as an antifungal medication. It's used to treat fungal infections around the eye, eyelids, cornea and (yes) the conjunctiva. Ah, the conjunctiva! So, it's a treatment for conjunctivitis! Hello, pink eye!

Let's open a joint called Pink Eye Pizza!

OK, all this to say, stay away from pre-shredded product. Natamycin is not going to hurt you. Neither is potato starch.

But it is going to hurt your pizza.

Because of the anti-coagulant coating on the shredded cheese, it has trouble melting. I've literally been served a pizza straight from the oven where the cheese looks like it just came out of the bag of shredded product. My wife and I were in a funky little novelty bar in a tourist town. And let me be clear: I love this bar as a bar. It's thoroughly authentic, inspired by locals and attractive to tourists. Unfortunately, as a dining establishment, this place is known for two things: its pizza and its gyro. We tried the pizza. When it arrived at our table, one look was all that was required to know the cheese was pre-shredded.

Instead of a layer of brown and bubbling molten cheese, there was a scattering of pale shreds. I lifted the crust and peeked at the bottom. It too was pale, and was pierced with a regular series of little holes. The holes are a telltale sign that the product is a pre-made pizza shell.

So really, what was going on here was the owner of the joint "known for its pizza" was provisioning from some big-box store where he bought giant boxes of pre-made shells, giant cans of pre-made sauce, giant bags of pre-shredded cheese, giant bags of pre-cut toppings, and had some pair of hired hands in the kitchen assembling pizzas and baking them until the timer bell rang.

It was not revolting.

But it was also memorable for the wrong reasons.

This is one of the reasons we are working to free the pizza.

This job of making pizza is not hard. But we've been convinced that it is. We're told it's the province of professionals in special uniforms who have magical skills bestowed upon them by corporate overlords or, in the case of celebrity pizzaioli, the highly selective and discriminating pizza gods of Mount Vesuvius. And then, after the big chains and the craft pizza icons, pizza gets corrupted by unambitious entrepreneurs whose only goal is to deliver a PLO. (Remember? The Pizza-Like Object.)

So, all this is a roundabout way of getting to the point of why we sneer at pre-shredded cheese.

Anyway, back to the story…

Low-moisture, whole-milk mozzarella.

THAT'S RIGHT: LOW-MOISTURE, WHOLE MILK MOZZARELLA

Do not be led astray by the part-skim version of the same product. The whole-milk version better facilitates the melting, eating and enjoying.

Why not fresh mozzarella? Because, hey, sometimes you see a commercial version of fresh mozzarella right there in the cheese case alongside the low-moisture product from a giant cheese-making monolith.

Here's the deal on fresh mozzarella. It's really good. It's also really wet. When baked onto a pizza, it doesn't brown well, and becomes kind of soupy and blotchy. It tastes great. It's good for certain kinds of pizzas and all kinds of other dishes. But it's not suitable for making a totally free, Americanized pizza.

I HAVE ACTUALLY MADE FRESH MOZZARELLA.

Like many other things, it is surprisingly easy once you get your hands on the right ingredients. You can't usually just walk into your supermarket and buy rennet, which is a required component for making cheese. It's a compound of enzymes that comes from the stomachs of ruminant animals (cows, sheep, goats, water buffalos, etc.). In layman's terms, it makes the molecules in the liquid milk clump into a solid cheese. I ordered rennet online, took a gallon of pasteurized whole milk, and made fresh mozzarella fairly quickly. It was not great, because you really need raw milk. But it looked and tasted like fresh mozzarella and was a sufficient experiment. I probably won't do it again soon.

Another challenge with fresh mozzarella is it can't be grated. It has to be applied to the pizza in slices or chunks. You don't get the uniform coverage that is an aesthetic of the great American pizza. You get the aforementioned soupy puddles. But low-moisture cheese can go up against the large holes in your grater and deliver the shreds required for optimum coverage across the pizza expanse. (Notice the word "optimum," not the word "maximum." Balance is required in all things here.)

HARD-AGED CHEESE IS EASY?

Once you've acquired your low-moisture, whole-milk mozzarella, you want to find a hard cheese. You'll be shredding this cheese with the fine holes on your grater. I recommend steering clear of the pre-packaged cheese section where you found the mozzarella, and slide on over to the deli. Some folks will send you in search of the gold-standard granddaddy of hard aged Italian cheese, Parmigiano

Reggiano. And yes, it's great cheese. It's also priced like gold. And personally, I prefer pecorino Romano or, in a pinch, sharp Provolone. It's less expensive and has a bigger, more funky flavor profile.

The sharp, salty, funky characteristics of these cheeses are a pungent contrast to the mellow, melty magic of the low-moisture mozzarella. It should be used in moderation, and it doesn't melt as well as mozzarella—but it tastes great. I call it the accent cheese. It's one of the things that helps give a professional pizza its edge over uninformed, home-baked pizza sadness. We want home-baked pizza gladness.

PREPARING LIKE A BOY SCOUT?

No, that is not a sexist, gender-driven simile. That is literally the Boy Scout motto: "Be Prepared." Maybe we should call this "Pizza Scouts." Anyway, here's the deal: I'm prepared to make a pizza at any time.

At this writing, in my freezer are nine dough balls of various compositions.

In my refrigerator is a container with a few ounces of sauce made from San Marzano tomatoes. I use San Marzanos when making pizza for special occasions and this is leftover from one such occasion. If I don't use it soon, it also goes in the freezer.

In my cold-cuts drawer are four packages of low-moisture, whole-milk mozzarella, about a quarter pound of pecorino Romano, and an array of cured meats.

Starting at zero with a frozen dough ball, I can throw down a fresh pizza in a couple of hours. Most of that time is passive prep, like waiting for the dough to thaw and the oven to heat. Considering that it can take about that long for a mediocre delivery pizza to arrive, which would you rather have?

Key in this spontaneous equation is the cheese.

The beauty of the low-moisture mozzarella is that it is shelf-stable for as long as six months. Fresh mozzarella, which has its own merits, is not so shelf stable. It typically must be used within a few days. It can be frozen, but the freezing of cheese is just so very aesthetically wrong. It comes out of the freezer as an abused version of its former self. And again, we're on a quest for a great American pizza. The fresh mozzarella product is for something else.

If you want to know how to go from frozen dough to fresh pizza in a couple of hours, we talk about that later in the Appendix. First, we have to make a fresh-dough pizza and all of the magic that comes with that.

PREPARING TO BAKE
IF YOU CAN'T STAND THE HEAT, TOO BAD.
THAT'S THE PRICE OF GREAT PIZZA

This is where it all begins to come together. You've made dough. You've made sauce. You've bought cheese. You've done this all with thought, purpose and intent. Time now to bring it all together in a delightfully flat flavor bomb.

TIMING IS EVERYTHING

Well, maybe not *everything*. But it's important. Making a pizza is a series of timings. Timing matters when making the dough. Timing matters when proofing the dough. And now, timing matters when removing the dough from the fridge and heating up your oven. It will also matter when baking. So, with that…

REMOVE THE DOUGH FROM THE FRIDGE

This is the first thing to do. If you don't do it first, you will forget. And forgetting is bad. If you ever try to stretch cold dough, you'll find that it's not fun. The glutens need to relax and get all pizza happy. That requires sitting at kitchen temperature for at least an hour. I usually give it more. When it reaches the ambient temperature of the kitchen, it's relaxed enough to be stretched easily.

How many dough balls should you take out?

That depends on how many pizzas you plan to make on your first pass. You might be thinking that this is an experiment, and you're going to start with one.

If that's how you're feeling, I'd recommend taking out two dough balls. Here's why: After the first one, you're going to be so amazed, you're going to need a second one just to be sure you really did it.

If you're doing this all by yourself, and not feeding anyone else, two pizzas sounds like a lot. It's not. Here's why: you will eat that first pizza in record time. You'll be so overwhelmed with the joy of your first foray into real, live homemade pizza subversion, you'll want another pizza.

You'll make that second pizza and take pictures of it, which you forgot to do on the first one. Then, you'll probably eat half. The rest will wrap up nicely in aluminum foil and sit in the fridge until breakfast, when you reheat it and eat it with a fried egg.

So take out at least one more dough ball than you think you need.

SET THE OVEN RACK

After removing your dough from the fridge and putting it on the counter, open your oven door. First, move the oven rack up to the top third of the oven. If your oven is electric, there should be about 4 inches between the shelf and the broiler element. If your oven is gas, there should be about 6 inches between the shelf and the broiler element.

Next, place your baking steel, cast iron pizza pan, or previously seasoned stone on that top rack. We've got it all up there because high heat is our friend.

There are a lot of pizza gurus out there, people who are much smarter than I am, telling you to put your oven rack at the lowest level, mere inches from the baking element. I have tried this. For me, it does not yield a satisfactory pizza. The bottom bakes too much. The top bakes not enough. The last time I tried it, I got a pizza that was like a cracker with tomato and cheese on it.

My top-rack methodology is based on years of non-scientific experimentation. I started by working on the middle rack. Then, for years, I used the upper middle. Now, as I've evolved to using the broiler, I've switched to using the upper rack. And frankly, it's consistently the best pizza to come out of my oven. It ranks up there with the pies that were coming out of my wood-fired oven when I had one and could stoke it to 900 degrees. (But trust me, nothing is ever going to be the same as a pizza baked in a 900-degree oven. It is transformative. If you want to investigate these ovens, we talk about them on the website.

SETTING THE OVEN TEMP

Back to your home oven. With your baking surface positioned on the rack as discussed, set the oven temperature as high as it goes. Most ovens I've used go to 550. Some go to only 525. I once owned a 1950s vintage gas range that went over 600. (I've heard of guys who disconnect the lock on the door of their self-cleaning ovens and bake pizzas at 900 degrees. For so many reasons unrelated to making a killer pizza, that's a bad plan. We're not going to entertain that idea here. Don't do it.)

The oven will probably take about half an hour to reach temperature.

THAT IS NOT HOT ENOUGH.

Sorry for yelling. The all caps is necessary. It's not enough that your oven is at temperature. Your baking surface also needs to be at temperature. It's a dense thermal mass that requires a lot of heating.

Once the oven reaches temperature, let your oven heat for an additional 60 minutes. One hour. 3,600 seconds. This hot, hot oven is the kind of thing that happens in a pizzeria, whether it's a professional joint or your joint.

Simple things like heat make a huge difference. Temperature means a lot. And when we're talking about making an American-style pizza using a Neapolitan-style dough, this 550-degree oven is going to be our friend. As we've discussed previously, true Neapolitan-style pizzas are soft and chewy and kinda wet.

We are not doing that.

We're using a somewhat lower temperature, which yields a crust with more structure, with satisfying crunch and a tasty char.

Once your new pizza oven has been getting all hot and happy, we're going to take on the greatest psychological challenge of all: stretching the dough.

THE JOY OF STRETCH

This is the part that freaks out people: stretching the dough and making an actual, round pizza. In reality, it's just not that hard. It only requires that you a) visualize a round, stretched dough and b) assume success.

You can do this.

Here's something else: You have permission to NOT toss the dough in the air. You also have permission to make a pizza that's not perfectly round. (Though making it round is a lot easier than it might seem.)

You have NO PERMISSION to use a rolling pin.

Does that seem didactic? Tyrannical? Pushy?

You are on your way to pizza heroism. You've done something most people will never do: You've created a living thing called pizza dough. And using a rolling pin takes that thing you've spent time kneading and nurturing and nullifies it.

The rolling pin does a couple of things. Most importantly, it is a crime against your dough. Pressing the dough with a rolling pin presses the gas out of the dough.

Degassing the dough leads to a dense, compact and unsatisfying crust. There's a big chain of beloved pizzerias that uses a machine called a sheeter. They feed the dough into the sheeter and it spits out a perfectly formed disc of dough ready for topping. And as a pizza, while it is round and cheesy, it's also not special. It's dense and uninteresting. It's popular not because the pizza is great, but because it's there, it's cheap, and you can have your pizza any way you want it.

Nobody goes to McDonald's and says, "These are the best burgers ever!" They go and get exactly what they expected and move on to the next thing on the to-do list.

Some people think the rolling pin will make the dough round for them. It won't. It just produces a flat, amoeba-shaped object.

No rolling pin. And if you have a sheeter (in the form of a pasta machine), forget that, too. We're going for transcendence.

You can do this. You can stretch a dough and make it round.

Ready?

Let's say you made six dough balls. That means we're making 12-inch pizzas. So, envision stretching a pizza to approximately 12 inches. (And know that nobody will be using a ruler here.)

HAVE YOUR PEEL READY.

Having a place waiting to accept your stretched dough helps your head. Put your peel somewhere out of the way where you're not going to smack the handle and send it flipping into the kitchen. (That's the voice of experience speaking.) Dust the surface with semolina or cornmeal. It doesn't need to obliterate the surface. We just need enough for it to act like a layer of ball bearings underneath a pizza that's been dressed for business. (Psychologically, this is another one of the hurdles in pizza making. There's a lot of fear happening here. "How will I get it off the peel?!" It wants to get off the peel. Simple physics is on your side. It wants to slide.)

DUST YOUR WORK SURFACE WITH FLOUR.

How much flour? That's a good question. I used to have a pile of it. Now, I use a lot less. It's a combination of experience and Yankee thrift. I hate wasting ingredients. But I recommend erring on the side of excess. Throw down a handful of all-purpose flour on your surface. I use a big cutting board, unless I'm working in a kitchen that has granite countertops. Then, I just work right on the stone.

Spread around enough flour that you have a swirly dusted surface with flour to spare.

ADDRESS THE DOUGH BALL.

It's sitting there, in its plastic bag, taunting you. You are about to show it who's boss. Unzip the bag and say, "Hello, ball!" (Somewhere out there, diehard fans of *The Honeymooners* are cursing my name.) Presumably, the ball is still small enough that you can reach inside and remove it gently. If not, if your dough ball has swollen to a size that makes removing it without deforming it a challenge, do what I do. Take a sharp knife (I use a serrated knife with a very pointy tip), and just slit the bag open from near bottom to top. Then, gently lift the dough ball from within.

PUT THE DOUGH BALL ON THE FLOURED SURFACE.

I once sat at the counter in a really busy, Neapolitan-style pizza joint and watched the pizzaiolo working his dough. He was turning and burning, making pizzas one after the other like there was no tomorrow. He would grab a dough ball, drop it onto the flour and firmly press it with the palm of his hand to form a thick disc.

Then, he would flatten it further by pressing it with both hands, rotating it and stretching it outward until it was about half an inch thick.

At this point, your dough ball for a 12-inch pizza might be about five to six inches in diameter.

This next step is something I've picked up along the way, and it does two things: One, it gives the edge of your crust, the *cornicione* (Italian for "cornice," or what is colloquially referred to in some places in the US as "the handle"), a defined place to happen. Two, it makes the edge of the pizza more clearly defined. (This may be a purely psychological tool. But I find it leads to some of my prettiest pizzas.)

Using your fingers, dimple a circle of dots into the dough about an inch from the edge. It's almost as if we're drawing a dotted line around the inner edge of the pizza.

See how nice and uniform that looks?

Next, using both hands, stretch the middle of the dough out some more until it starts to get wide enough that it feels like you can pick it up with both hands and get underneath it.

Important tip: This dough is resilient and stretchy. You might fear tearing a hole in it. That could happen. But it really needs to stretch a lot before you can rip it or put a finger through it. And if that happens, it is easily fixed.

Now that we have a floppy disc of dough, there are various ways to proceed. Professionals all have different techniques. The one that I have used most and recommend is "knuckling it."

When the dough is stretched thin and flat enough, you can make two fists and get your knuckles underneath the edge of the disc. Stretch it with your knuckles until you feel like it's getting thin enough in the center that you're concerned. You're going to notice that the outer part of the dough is still somewhat thicker. Now, I grab the edge of the dough with both hands, almost like a steering wheel. Stretch the outer portion. Feel free to let gravity help you with this.

And no, this is not sexy. You probably want to be tossing the dough spinning into the air.

Don't be tempted. (Yet.) There should be no drama in stretching your pizza dough. We are not looking for "flair." We are looking not for sexy dough throwing, but for a sexy pizza that makes your diners' eyes roll back in their heads.

Using both hands on the wheel, stretch the edge of the dough until you've got a disc that's about 12 inches in diameter. It might be smaller. It might be larger. But it will be about a foot across. And it should be roundish. We'll know how round when we put it down on the peel.

PLACE THE PIZZA DOUGH ON THE PEEL.

Is it round-ish? Great. If it's not round-ish enough, here's a crazy tip: Rearrange it until it is. Seriously. This option seems to escape a lot of people who are making pizza shaped like an amoeba. Just arrange the dough on the peel, gently pulling or pushing the edges until it's round enough that you feel like you've accomplished something.

And while we're at it, to give you confidence in the little ball bearings underneath the pizza, pick up the peel and give it a little horizontal shake. See how the dough slides on the surface of the peel? Physics!

But be warned: this will not last indefinitely. If the pizza sits on the peel for too long, you have a challenge. You're working in a hot kitchen, you're putting toppings on a flimsy sheet of dough, and that dough is eventually going to get soft and absorb those ball bearings. Figure you have 10 minutes, tops, to get that pizza into the oven.

Next up: sauce and cheese.

GETTING BAKED

CREATING THE JOY THAT IS HOMEMADE PIZZA

Are you ready? Can you stand the anticipation? This is it: Where it all comes together. You've made dough. You've made sauce. You've bought cheese. You've done this all with thought, purpose and intent. Now the oven is hotter than hot. You've stretched your dough. Time to bring it all together in a delightfully flat flavor bomb.

"WHERE DID IT GO?!"

In cooking, there is an important French expression: *Mise en place*. Loosely translated, it means "everything in its place." It's about having all of your ingredients and tools where they need to be.

This is vitally important for making pizza—even more so if you have a tiny kitchen. My own kitchen used to be enormous. I was pretty good at *mise en place*. When we sold that house and moved into a 26-foot RV, I learned *mise en place* like *il n'ya pas de demain* ("there is no tomorrow").

Granted, I wasn't making a lot of pizza in that RV, though I did have a wood-pellet-fired portable pizza oven in one of the storage compartments. But working in that tiny little kitchen was an exercise in organization.

When the pandemic hit, we decided to move into our income property, a rental condo at the base of a ski resort. Compared to the RV, that kitchen was palatial: 64 square feet, and roughly the footprint of a Mazda Miata. The appliances and cabinets took up most of that space. The remaining 24 square feet is floor space, meaning just about everything is within reach—and there's little enough counter space that I need to be organized. (And the oven is an old beater—proving that as long as it's functioning, any home oven will do.)

I have learned *mise en place* as never before. You should, too. Before you start cooking, there should be a place for everything, everything should be in its place, and it should be organized in small bowls, pinch bowls, saucers, or whatever other containers you use. All tools should be handy. You should know where everything is. (It takes a little practice. But once you get good at it, you won't think twice about saying, "Hey, let's make a pizza!") There's a photo of my *mis* for a three-pizza night on the website.

We're going to take our stretched dough, apply sauce and cheese, make sure it slides on the peel, then put it in the oven and bake it—using the broiler—for about six minutes. In a very specific order, here are the steps we're about to take:

GETTING SAUCED

Once again, no measurements here. Don't get freaked out. Just have confidence in your ability to judge your pizza based on the description here, combined with your life experience in the land of pizza.

You've stretched your dough and placed it on the peel. It is somewhat round, if not perfectly so. (You may have surprised even yourself.)

Using a big spoon or ladle, spread a thin layer of sauce around the pizza. If you're making a 14-inch pizza, that's probably no more than 1/2 a cup. For a 12-inch pizza, that's a third of a cup. Probably less. It's going to depend on the thickness of your sauce. I use a ladle that holds about half a cup of sauce, and that's usually sufficient. Smaller pizzas take less, obviously. If you've ever watched a pizzaiolo in a pizza joint assemble a pizza, you can still see the white dough through the red sauce. The sauce is not opaque. It's like a window into the pizza's future. Yet, to the uninitiated watching this process, it always seems like that amount of sauce is too little to give the rich tomato goodness you're getting in the final analysis.

As I'm writing this, there's a national TV commercial playing in my head. It's for a national chain of pizza joints, and it shows a pizza being assembled. The thick, red sauce is being spread with a trowel, yielding a thick, red layer of mortar like they're going to be cementing pizzas together for building a wall. Yes, it might visually convey a sense of richness. But it will not yield a good pizza. It will be heavy and sloppy and not magical like yours will be.

Again, use little enough sauce that you can still see the dough through the sauce. You do not want so much sauce that it's opaque. In the land of pizza making, as in so many other places, less is more.

Spread the sauce around the dough out to the edges. I know one guy, a multi-millionaire with distinctive and dismissive opinions about everyone and everything, who likes to make pizza. He insists that the edge of the pizza, what becomes the *cornicione* (you know, the handles) is a waste and pizzerias are stingy, robbing him of valuable pizza goodness to save mere pennies. When he makes his own pizza, he takes the sauce all the way to the very edge. I do not recommend this. Besides the simple fact that you lose a convenient place to hold a piping hot slice of pizza, it also robs you of the important and satisfying aesthetic of having made a proper pizza. The *cornicione* is not wasteful. It is tradition. At the end of the day, pizza is a bread. And a bread has a crust. Do not be like the greedy, unpleasant rich man who gives multi-millionaires a bad name. Take your sauce as far as you want, but give yourself just enough edge to have some unsauced joy at the end of your slice. It's going to feel good and taste even better.

GETTING CHEESED

When the sauce is spread out to the edge of the disc, it's time to add the mozzarella. As with the sauce on the dough, which provides a peek at the pizza dough below, you do not want to obliterate the red of the sauce with the white of the cheese. You still want to be able to see red sauce peeking through the cheese.

Sprinkle the mozzarella on the sauce until you have good, consistent coverage, but you can still see a fair amount of red peeking through. I find that on a 12-inch pizza, this means a big, generous handful of shredded low-moisture mozzarella. Maybe the size of a tennis ball. If we were to measure it, it would be half to two-thirds of a cup. If you're unsure, err on the side of caution.

Once the mozzarella is spread, pinch a generous clump of shredded Romano with your fingers. Hold your hand about two feet above the pizza and sprinkle it around. (Seriously, the height makes a difference. Your brain works your fingers better.) If that isn't quite enough Romano, if you don't make it all the way around, grab a little more to finish the job. It might be about two tablespoons, but don't get hung up on the amount. Just get it on there.

Guess what: **You now have a pizza that is ready to bake.**

Now, this next tip can save a lot of anxiety.

Pick up the peel with your pizza on it, and give it a little, horizontal shake.

Is the pizza still sliding on your semolina or cornmeal ball bearings? Excellent. It will slide off the peel and into the oven easily.

Is the pizza not sliding? Does it seem as one with the peel? Easily fixed.

Holding up the peel near your face, lightly pinch the dough nearest you using your thumb and index finger. **Lift the pizza dough a little bit, and blow a puff of air under the pizza.**

You should see the whole pizza puff up just a little bit, then settle back.

Once again, try giving the peel a little, horizontal shake. Does the pizza slide now? Perfect. If not, try puffing again.

Dough stuck to the peel is an annoying little bugaboo. Fortunately, it is easily overcome with a little puff of your breath. Just so long as you haven't left the dough on the peel for too long, you should be good.

STEP-BY-STEP PHOTOS OF HOW TO MAKE A PIZZA

If you go to the website at the following address, you will find a page that includes these photos in color, along with a real-time video of this exact pizza being assembled. There's a video of this at the website, www. FreeThePizza.com/video

Flatten the dough ball on your work surface

Once the disc is flat enough to be workable, dimple the inside edge

Stretch dough until you can get your knuckles under it, and continue
stretching

Once dough is very thin in the middle, grip outer edge and continue
stretching

A 6-ounce dough ball yields a 10-inch pizza. Put down dough and arrange into a round.

Slide onto peel and apply thin layer of sauce

Sprinkle shredded mozzarella, just enough so red sauce is still peeking through

Sprinkle two generous pinches of shredded hard cheese

LAUNCHING

Go to your lovely hot, 550-degree oven. You want to be able to see this as it happens. We're going to be putting the peel inside the oven and sliding it out from under our pizza as the pizza slides onto the baking surface.

Momentum is everything here. You don't need a lot. But hesitating doesn't help.

Face the oven, and open the door with your free hand.

Put the peel into the oven at a slight angle. The tip of the peel should be near the back of the baking surface.

Give the peel a little skootch forward. The pizza should begin sliding off.

In the same motion, just slide the peel backwards and out. Understand, with the peel at an angle and the pizza atop those tiny, natural ball bearings of corn meal or semolina, the pizza would really rather leave the peel and be in the oven.

So, slip the peel out and let the pizza slide onto the baking surface.

Close the oven door.

Turn the oven's temperature control to high BROIL.

Set your timer for three minutes.

It has begun.

If you can, go ahead and watch your pizza transform through the glass of the oven window. It will gradually begin to puff and bubble, until it becomes fully engaged and active.

Yay, thermodynamics!

GAS VS. ELECTRIC OVENS

This is important.

Your oven doesn't care. It is not necessarily designed to cooperate with your desire to make pizza. You are going to get to experiment a little here.

ELECTRIC: Most electric ovens seem to have a thermostat that turns off the broiler when the oven is at 500 degrees.

Accordingly, to get the broiler in your electric oven to go on, you'll need to keep the oven door ajar. The baking surface will remain hot enough to make the dough pop, and the cooling oven will let the broiler go on.

Once the broiler goes on, close the door.

I've used some electric ovens where the door need not be kept ajar. It's going to be a trial and error thing for each oven.

GAS: Most of the gas ovens I've used do not present this challenge. The gas broiler goes on and stays on. They are some of the best ovens I've used for pizza. And in some cases, I've used ovens where the gas broiler won't go on unless the oven door is shut.

BOTTOM BROILER: If you've got a bottom broiler in a drawer beneath the oven, that presents other challenges. I've tried to make pizza in these and it's not fun. My recommendation is to bake the pizza in the top of the oven without attempting the broiler. It's a compromise, but your pizza will still be quite good. It'll just take longer. Figure you will as much as double the baking time. Watch the browning of the crust. That will be your cue for when it's ready to rotate, and when it's fully baked.

At three minutes, open the oven door. If you're using two peels, one wood and one metal, now's the time to get the metal peel.

Slip your peel under the pizza to give it a spin. Using your fingers but without burning yourself, gingerly and quickly rotate the pizza 180 degrees, then slide it back onto the baking surface.

Close the door, and set the timer for three more minutes.

Every minute or so, peek at the pizza. You may need to remove it before the three minutes are up.

If it has a little char on it, with little black bubbles appearing around the edge of the crust, that's good. Char is flavor, and it's an indicator that your oven is hot enough.

Warning: If you don't monitor the progress, you could end up with Satan's own communion wafer.

Retrieve the pizza. When the time is up (or when the pizza is fully baked with a little char on it), remove it from the oven by sliding the peel beneath it and pulling it out of the oven.

Place it on a cutting board or a pizza tray. It's also probably molten, swimming in dangerously hot lethal cheese and sauce. Let it rest for a moment, until it begins to set. Then, using your pizza cutter (or a chef's knife), cut the pizza into four or six slices.

Congratulations. You have a classic cheese pizza! Pretty cool, hunh? It's pretty as a picture and tastes even better. And you had the power to do it. You are a pizza subversive.

If you're going to bake another pizza, switch the oven from BROIL back to BAKE at 550. You want it to stay at temperature while you enjoy your first pizza.

STRETCH, TOP, BAKE, REPEAT!

Are you going to make another pizza? Repeat the process.

- Stretch the dough
- Apply the sauce
- Sprinkle the cheeses
- Launch the pie
- Broiler on
- 3-minute timer
- Rotate the pizza

- Another 3-minute timer
- Monitor the progress
- Retrieve
- Return the oven to 550 bake
- Let pizza set
- Cut
- Eat
- Repeat

WHAT'S THAT? YOU WANT TOPPINGS?

No problem. Add toppings on the next pizza if you like. And remember: Less is more. We'll talk about additional toppings in the next chapter.

WANT PRINTABLE CHEATSHEETS OF ALL THESE STEPS TO USE IN THE KITCHEN?

Check out the website. There are PDF downloads at

www.FreeThePizza.com/cheatsheets

TOPPING ON TOPPING ACTION!

Why have we waited until after making a cheese pizza to begin talking toppings? That's simple: it's better to get the basics wired before moving on to more. Once you feel how a pizza works, then the more complex topic of toppings comes into play.

And by the way, toppings are indeed complex. How much is too much? What can you get away with? What goes together? What's a huge mistake? Wherefore pineapple?

Alright. Pineapple. Is it so wrong that it's right? Why is it so polarizing? Have the people who hate it ever actually tried it? Or do they just wear their hate for the idea of it on their sleeves?

But I have a better question…

What made a guy in Canada say, "I'm going to put pineapple and back bacon on a pizza and call it Hawaiian"? Because yes, Hawaiian pizza is reported to be a Canadian invention. Let's forget for a moment that if I were asked to imagine a Hawaiian pizza, I probably would have ditched the back bacon (known among Americans as Canadian bacon) for SPAM. Hawaiians love their SPAM, and it would cook up better on a pizza, I think. Or kalua pork, the Hawaiian version of pulled-pork barbecue. Maybe small pieces of pineapple, sliced thin. Or crushed pineapple, pre-cooked to make it less wet. Dunno. Have to try it. I've tried other things that seem a little crazy, which is how I've gotten to things like my pizza called "A Race With The Devil On A Spanish Highway." More on that later, if you're lucky. Along with more on pineapple. I have a fresh pineapple sitting here by my computer as I write this. I don't hate pineapple; I just don't see the need for it. But since it's a favorite topping for some, I'm experimenting with it. I've had commercial Hawaiian pizza, and it lacks finesse. Big chunks of wet pineapple. Dry Canadian bacon, which is an uninteresting meat product. If we want to honor Hawaii with a pizza let's do better, eh?

TOPPING PHILOSOPHY

As with the sauce and the cheese, less is more. It might seem like a good idea to make a Meat Lover's Mega Pizza covered in 16 ounce ribeye steaks.

I dare you to pick up a slice.

You're going to have a serious, greasy mess on your hands.

If you want to go whole hog with toppings (Roast Pig Pizza, an entire suckling pig with an apple in its mouth!), you can get adventurous—after you have learned how to grapple with the basics.

Despite some of the meat-laden things you may have been served from a commercial pizzeria, loading a pizza with slabs of meat is a challenge. Making it work, especially as a home pizzaiolo, takes patience, practice and perseverance. It's possible your first attempt will be filled with cheese and regret and you will have a calzone on your hands. (If you don't know what a calzone is, think of it like a pizza that is folded in half before baking.) I call this class of pizza "Danger Pie." The first time I tried a Danger Pie was in my wood-fired oven. We had a lot of meat toppings left over, and a guest who loved meat. So I took a chance.

I ended up scraping meat and cheese off the deck of the oven. What I had to serve was, well, not much of a pizza. More like a meat, cheese and grease pudding.

THE CLEARLY COMPOSED PIZZA

A composed dish is something that has been put together with a thoughtful plan. You often hear the word "composed" to describe certain salads. Judges on TV cooking competition shows love when they are served what they call, "a composed dish."

When making pizza, composure is your friend in both food and demeanor. Assuming success, pacing yourself, using discretion, pretending you know what you're doing, and using confidence to make pizza and impress people—all of these things pay off.

USE TOPPINGS RESPONSIBLY AND IN MODERATION.

Remember, we're freeing the pizza, not burying it. Please, use toppings sparingly. You'll be much happier.

You'll probably also be happier when we use the "P" word: Pepperoni!

Here now, the sometimes surprising list of America's Top Ten Favorite Pizza Toppings, and the Free The Pizza editorial commentary thereupon. I cannot tell you who generated this list. It's all over the internet in dozens of blog posts and articles without any attribution. Ready?

1. Pepperoni

On the eighth day, apparently, God created the pepperoni. And it was good. This seems to be America's favorite pizza topping. I'm betting one reason it's a top fave is because the word "pepperoni" sounds Italian. But if you ordered a pepperoni pizza in Italy, they'd look at you funny, then make you a pizza with little peppers on it. Pepperoni is an American invention.

2. Mushrooms

This was just a little surprising. I didn't expect to see America embracing the lowly mushroom. You don't see a lot of "I [heart] fungi" bumper stickers. I happen to enjoy mushrooms, especially with spicy Italian sausage. I like using Crimini mushrooms, also known as Baby Bella. It's a brown mushroom that looks (as the latter name implies) like a little portabella mushroom. But really, it's the same as the standard white mushroom. It's just brown because it's been harvested at a slightly more mature stage. They taste a little earthier.

3. Onions

What's not to love? Thinly sliced white onions are a welcome addition to many different pizzas. Some folks enjoy caramelized red onions. (Just sauté them in a pan until they start to caramelize, then take them aside for topping your pizza at will.) My wife loves onions, but finds caramelized red onions too sweet. One of my new favorite toppings is chopped scallions, sprinkled on top of the pizza after it's baked. Besides the herbal fresh pop of the stems and the mellower onion taste, it also looks bright and fresh.

4. Sausage

For my money, this is the #1 meat topping. I prefer it to pepperoni, as it has a more complex flavor, especially if it's a really good artisan Italian sausage. As mentioned above, one of my go-to pizzas is sausage and mushroom. I remember, years ago, making my first sausage and mushroom pizza, taking a bite, and thinking, "Damn, I'd pay money for this."

5. Bacon

This shouldn't come as a surprise. If I had to guess why it's not #1, I'd say it's probably because it's not already cooked. It's not as easy as a ready-to-eat meat like pepperoni. Using bacon effectively on a pizza requires par-cooking it. Otherwise, it either ends up flaccid and fatty, or it renders bacon fat all over the pizza. Still, an excellent topping.

6. Extra Cheese

This just seems gratuitous. There should be enough cheese to strike a balance with the rest of the toppings. Extra cheese throws that balance off and can lead to a limp, sloppy pie. But to each his own. I don't recommend it.

7. Black Olives

My wife hates olives. I love them—but not the kind that you typically see in a standard American pizza joint, which is a rubbery and bland, sliced black product with a hole in it and comes out of a can. I prefer a whole olive, traditionally cured, that still has the pit. Call it a holdover from my salad days as a sailing bum eating pizza in the Mediterranean. Olives that still have the pit taste better, as the brine hasn't penetrated the entire olive. Sometimes, I throw them on the pizza whole, with the pit. Other times, I pit them first. (It's easy. Just smack the olive with the side of a heavy knife and pop out the pit.) Warning: Use them whole with the pit, and when you launch the pizza, there's a good chance they'll roll off. Be careful. You can try pressing them gently into the pizza so they're stable. Or add them after the pizza is on the baking surface.

8. Green Peppers

This is an example of a habit inspired by commerce. Green bell peppers are cheap. I almost never buy green bell peppers anymore. What's the point? They're bitter, un-ripened red bell peppers. (The rest of the civilized world wonders why Americans love their green bell peppers.) I spend the extra money and buy red bell peppers. But to each his own. Whether you prefer green or red, here's the caution on bell peppers: They contain a lot of moisture. Before using them on a pizza, you might want to cook them a bit on the stove and get rid of some of that moisture. As a pizza-making lawyer friend likes to say, "Moisture is the enemy." I often cook bell peppers until they're flaccid. Sometimes, I roast them or grill them and peel off the skins.

9. Pineapple

You might consider pineapple to be the top crime against pizza. But hey, we're just reporting the facts. Pineapple is the ninth favorite pizza topping in the US. (Nobody asked me.) I was originally thinking that it's outside the purview of this guide to opine upon the Pineapple Problem. But perhaps it's time to reevaluate. I should take my own advice re pizza snobbery, to wit: It's just silly. As mentioned near the beginning of this chapter, we might experiment with some fresh pineapple. Stay tuned…

10. Spinach

This came as a surprise. I use spinach on pizza with some frequency. I was just unaware that many others were fans. I put spinach together with bacon for a pizza crowd-pleaser that surprises people. Though, some gourmets will likely call me subversive on this count: I use frozen spinach. I always have it handy, and I think it stands up better to the rigors of baking than does its fresh counterpart. However, I always let the frozen spinach thaw, then squeeze out the excess water first.

That's the list of America's Favorites. I have three other favorite toppings that did not make the list. Ready?

. . .

11. Shrimp

Nobody ever sees shrimp coming. You serve shrimp on a pizza, and the reaction is, "What?!" My fondness for shrimp on pizza goes back to the aforementioned days of Mediterranean pizza. The *pizza pescatore* (fisherman's pizza) would come with whole clams, whole mussels, and a whole prawn or langouste. Yes, it's cumbersome. You have to shell the animal at the table with a knife and fork while you're eating a pizza. And the disembodied prawn head stares at you for the rest of the meal. But it's tasty. On my own pizzas, I usually use EZ-peel frozen shrimp and peel it before baking. When I can find it, I use rock shrimp or Argentine red shrimp, both of which have a rich taste that hints of lobster. Otherwise, I just use whatever white shrimp is handy. I try to get wild caught. I always look for medium size, or small if available as uncooked. If I'm stuck with large or XL shrimp, I cut them into smaller pieces. It's unwieldy to put giant shrimp on a pizza you're cutting up and serving to a group of people. Whole shrimp in the shells with their heads are dramatic and flavorful, but inconvenient. And you know someone's going to get squeamish. I'd normally say, "Too bad!" But the intent here is not to alienate anyone. I'll happily use whole, unshelled giant shrimp when I'm dining alone. And maybe some olives. (My wife just sees the olives on a pizza and knows she can't eat it. They've contaminated everything on top.)

12. Chopped Garlic

Though I never had it back then, I remember this being a staple menu item in some pizzerias when I was a kid. So a few years ago, I tried it on my own pizza. People loved it. So why the heck not? And it pairs well with shrimp. People seem to have a sense of shrimp and garlic as a decadent combination and who am I to argue?

. . .

13. Fresh Hot Peppers

This started years ago when my wife and I were living in Los Angeles. We were in our favorite dive bar and saw the cook eating his lunch: He'd made a pizza topped with pepperoni and sliced fresh jalapeños. The bright green pepper slices looked so good we ordered pepperoni and jalapeño pizza ourselves. Since then, I've experimented with lots of different peppers. When they're in season, Hatch chilis are fun. My fallback peppers, though, are serrano and Fresno peppers. They have bite, they're colorful, and they liven up a pizza. I usually slice them and cook them on the pizza. Once in a while I spread the slices raw on a freshly baked pizza.

YOU MUST LIMIT YOURSELF TO THESE TOPPINGS AND NO OTHERS!

Of course not. Please. The rules of pizza are few. Aside from the laws to be followed for baking efficacy, you can do just about anything you want. Even the pineapple thing, as annoying as it is, has its place. Personally, I've done all kinds of crazy pizza experiments, including topping a pizza with leftover gumbo. (It was really good. But how often do you have leftover gumbo around when you're ready to make pizza?)

There are lots of classic pizzas that we're not addressing here. They're more "fancy" and Neapolitan than they are American in their bearing. For example, the *pizza quatro stagioni* is an Italian classic. It's sectioned into quarters. Each section's toppings represent one of the year's four seasons. Winter has prosciutto and olives, spring is artichoke hearts, summer is tomatoes and basil, and mushrooms stand in for autumn. It's a lovely pizza if you're eating it by yourself. It's difficult to prepare one of these for a group of people that includes kids. "What's that pale green thing?!" "An artichoke heart." "Why are there leaves?!" "That's basil." "Why didn't you cook the bacon?!" "That's not bacon. It's prosciutto." "I hate olives!" Sigh. It's a lovely pizza to eat alone or with another person who shares your palate.

Similarly, we've not addressed the fabled *pizza Margherita*. It's just a simple cheese pizza with fresh basil on it. I make it a lot. It's great for a photo opp. It's a classic that some people adore. But I've found that, on the whole, the response to a Margherita is underwhelming. People seem to like the idea of it more than the actual experience of it.

There's a whole spectrum of pizzas from classic to crazy. We can't even begin to cover it all here. If you want to look at the menu from California Pizza Kitchen and plagiarize away, that's your choice. I think you're going to be making a better tasting pizza than any chain store product. I personally find BBQ chicken pizza to be a problem. But this is all about your personal preferences. At the core, it's still about one thing: taking back the pizza. Learning the simple craft of assembling dough, sauce and cheese for an extraordinary effect.

Again, my recommendation is to get your simple pizzas dialed in before you start slinging the toppings. Once you can bake a cheese pizza with confidence, climbing on top of the toppings is much easier. Dealing with the idiosyncrasies of fatty or wet toppings takes some practice. And when you cross your fingers and take a chance on trying something new, your chances for success and a crowd-pleasing pizza become greatly enhanced.

PIZZA COMBOS

It seemed wrong to talk about "pizza recipes," because that suggests something different than what's going to happen in this chapter. This is more about taking the recipe you've got for pizza and applying various topping combinations. So I wrote "Pizza Combos." Then, I immediately thought of the salty snack food by Mars, Inc., known officially as Combos Stuffed Snacks. It's comprised of a cracker tube stuffed with some kind of filling. There's a pizza-flavored Combo, of course. And there was an ad campaign some years back, the Man Mom campaign. The premise was: Combos are what your mom would serve you if your mom was a guy.

I don't think so. I think it would be actual pizza. All the time, in fact. But maybe that's just me.

Anyway, below are a few of my personal favorite topping combinations. They make for a well-composed pizza and have been shown to make people happy. Again: MY personal favorites. You will likely have others. Once you've mastered the basics and see how a well-composed pizza happens, there's an entire world of tantalizing toppings at your fingertips.

NOTE: Everything here is intended to be put on top of a red sauce pizza made with low-moisture mozzarella and Romano cheeses. There's no white pizza, no traditional Neapolitan pizzas, no pizza marinara for the vegans, just good ol' crowd-pleasing, red and white pizzas.

ANOTHER NOTE: All baking times here are predicated on the standard 6-minute baking cycle under a broiler in a 550-degree oven. However, your baking times may vary. Especially when you have a lot of toppings, your bake time may increase. Remember: It's OK to have some char on the crust. That's how you know it's getting good. You might find that the char on some of these is a bit more as the toppings get their due under the broiler.

PEPPERONI

No, technically not a combo. Yes, the granddaddy demigod of American pizza worship. When I'm looking for something easy, I go right to the packaged cold cuts section in the supermarket and buy sliced pepperoni. Yes, it's pre-cut. Yes, it's a mass-produced product. Yes, I'm going to make someone even more incredulous by saying: I also buy the store brand. Here's why: It actually tastes better. I did a non-scientific taste test comparison with several people. I had the big name brand and the national store brand. Every participant in the taste test agreed: The store brand was a better tasting product. But ultimately, it's going to depend on your store's store brand.

If I'm looking for a more upscale pepperoni, I look for any of the craft brands that are available in the deli area for about twice the price. They're really good. If the store doesn't have anything that high-end, I'll look for the big national deli brand that comes whole, and slice it myself. But overall, pepperoni seems to be a bit like bacon: No matter how cheap it is, it's all pretty good.

When you're putting pepperoni on a pizza, avoid the temptation to obliterate the cheese from view. It's tempting to cover the entirety of a pizza with pepperoni placed edge to edge. Avoid that temptation. Yes, you've seen it in commercial pizza. If you've ever had one of those pizzas, you may have noticed how paper-thin those pepperoni slices are. You are not going to accomplish that with the pepperoni available to you. If you try with more thickly-sliced pepperoni, you're going to have a mess on your hands. Fat will render out of that pepperoni until the pizza is swimming in orange grease.

Use enough pepperoni to make the pizza attractive without suggesting you have a pepperoni fetish. I just went and found a photo of one of my successful pepperoni pizzas. That 14-inch pizza had 19 slices of pepperoni on top. That's plenty, especially considering that the diameter of that pepperoni was about an inch and a half. With one-inch pepperoni, clearly you could add more.

How to make it: Obtain your pepperoni. If it's whole, slice it in advance (and make the slices thin). You don't want to have to be grabbing a whole sausage and a knife while you're in the throes of making a pizza. After you've made your cheese pizza, distribute your pepperoni in an attractive manner about the pie. Bake as usual.

PEPPERONI & ONION

One of my personal favorite combinations. It also comes with another warning: Beware the moisture monster. Onion has a lot of water in it. I like to take half an onion and slice it very thin. Not only does it mean less moisture per slice, but the moisture has an opportunity to cook out during baking. And cutting the onion into delicate, half-circle slices looks really good with the full-moon pepperoni.

I generally use a yellow onion, sometimes a sweet onion, and a red onion is always an option. I always cut more than I need. The onion slices get distributed between the pepperoni slices so, again, they're enough to be attractive but not overwhelming the pizza.

How to make it: Cut off the ends of an onion. Place the onion on end and slice it in half. Turn the half on its side, and slice very thin layers off the end. Slice more than you think you'll need. Break the onion layers apart. Once you've topped your pizza with pepperoni, distribute the onions like parentheses all about the pepperoni. Use enough to be attractive, not enough to overwhelm.

PEPPERONI & HOT PEPPERS

Around here, we love this pizza. The combination that started it all was pepperoni and jalapeño. You can do that if you like. I've been using serrano peppers because they're smaller and typically pack a little more heat. (Heat is all relative. I've eaten some jalapeños that were stunning in their intensity. It all depends on what you end up with.) I've also been on a Fresno chili kick lately. In my experience, they're normally hotter than jalapeños, and the red color looks great. My personal preference is a combination of serrano and Fresno.

How to make it: Have some sliced peppers at the ready. I find that, for general audiences, one serrano and one Fresno, each thinly sliced, are sufficient. Even my Irish-complected friends seem to be able to make that work without too much fanning of their mouths. Have the sliced peppers at the ready. Once the pepperoni have been distributed in your previously determined attractive manner, sprinkle the sliced peppers in and around. Proceed to the oven and launch.

ITALIAN SAUSAGE

At some point, we each get locked into our pepperoni habit. It becomes an unthinking, automatic response to fall back on the fabled pepperoni. No doubt, it's a combination of salt, fat and spices that just makes people feel like they're getting it done. But here's the deal: Sausage is not only a good alternative in the salt/fat/spice department, it's got a richer, more unctuous flavor profile. I now prefer it to pepperoni.

There's a local brand of hot Italian sausage that I love to use. It does not come as a bulk product, only as cased sausage links. So, I buy the links and remove the casing. Since this sausage is raw, it needs to be broken down into small enough bits that it will cook through. Taking a sharp knife, I slice the uncased link length wise, then do the same to each half. Then, I slice it crossways so I have little chunks of sausage that are about half an inch on all sides. The meat will stick to the knife and itself, so you have to be patient. But I've found that this size cooks up well, gets sufficiently caramelized, and is a total pleasure.

Some pizzamakers will tell you to par cook the sausage beforehand. That's a cautionary measure born of the epic Raw Pork Fear. We are using a hot enough oven and small enough pieces that par cooking shouldn't be necessary. (We'll save that step for the raw bacon.)

How to make it: Have the broken-down sausage at the ready. Once you've assembled your cheese pizza, distribute the sausage much as you would the pepperoni: with discretion. You may not use all the sausage you have on hand. Give the sausage bits even distribution and room to breathe. Better to use too little than too much. Once the pie has been sausaged, launch accordingly. Be careful, as sausage bits will attempt to escape the pizza upon launching…

SAUSAGE & MUSHROOM

I know people that will not touch the mushroom. Their loss. This pizza has grown on me. I used to be apathetic about mushrooms on pizza. Making this pizza myself made me realize just how flavorful and umami a pizza can be. I like to use crimini mushrooms, also called cremini or baby bella. If all you can find is white mushrooms, so be it. Depending on the size of the mushrooms, I typically use two to three on a 14-inch pizza. Slice the mushroom comfortably thin, stem and all. On a 14-inch pizza, I usually end up with about two dozen slices, and have a few left over. Sometimes, I'll chop them up into mushroom bits. (This is actually a good tactic when confronted with picky eaters who see a mushroom slice and say, "Ick!" Ask them if they'll eat mushrooms if they can't see them and they taste like meat. That's better than violating their trust and sneaking them in there—which I've also done and it always makes the victory feel unclean. Pizza is about joy. And integrity.)

How to make it: Once you've made your cheese pizza and applied the sausage in the appropriately attractive and discretionary manner, apply the mushroom slices in an equally attractive and discretionary manner. If using chopped mushrooms, sprinkle them evenly about the pizza. Launch.

BACON

This is a no-brainer. We live in the age of the bacon fetish. Even some vegans will covertly partake of bacon. Benjamin Franklin once said that "Beer is proof God loves us and wants us to be happy." Arguably, bacon works in that sentiment as well. So, get bacon. Any sliced bacon will do. (We're talking American style bacon, or what our friends from the British Commonwealth countries call "streaky bacon." No back bacon or so-called Canadian bacon. If you want to use that, you might as well just fall back to ham.)

Take three slices of bacon and fry them in a pan until they're about halfway to three quarters cooked, but not yet crisp. You want the fat to render out so you don't end up serving that on your pizza. Generally speaking, the white fat will have started turning brown. Pull the bacon out of the pan and drain it on paper towel. Once it's cool, cut the strips into one-inch pieces. Set aside for use.

How to make it: Assemble your cheese pizza. Apply the bacon squares with finesse and discretion. Extend your pinky in the air if that helps. You want bacon squares placed (yes) attractively. Launch the pizza and tell the room that bacon is forthcoming. They will applaud mightily. (It is a phenomenon of our time.)

BACON & SPINACH

This pizza is the crowd-pleasing surprise of the year. As stated previously, I'm something of a heretic in that I use frozen chopped spinach. I take about one third of a 12-ounce bag of frozen spinach and let it thaw. Then, I put it into a sheet of paper towel, roll it up, and squeeze it out over the sink. Green water will issue forth. I squeeze it out, then put the oppressed spinach into a bowl for standby. As for the bacon, follow the steps above for the straight bacon pizza.

How to make it: Bring your cheese pizza once again. Then, sprinkle the chopped spinach evenly around the pizza. Follow that with the bacon squares. You want them on the top so they get to revel in an abundance of cooking heat. Launch the pizza and again tell the room that bacon is forthcoming. They will again applaud mightily.

SHRIMP & GARLIC

This is the pizza they never see coming. My 14-inch pizza usually requires about a dozen medium shrimp. When I'm using frozen shrimp, I thaw and peel. Already peeled? Just remove the tail. No tail? No further prep. As for the garlic, I have a pretty heavy hand there. Two to three cloves, peeled and chopped small. Know that this pizza will be a little bit wet. That's one reason to not use too many shrimp. I've tried par-cooking the shrimp, and that doesn't seem to help much.

How to make it: You've assembled your cheese pizza. Place the shrimp strategically and attractively. Sprinkle the garlic evenly around the pie. Launch, bake and enjoy the resulting thrill.

Options: All kinds of things happen to this pizza. Sometimes, some chili peppers end up on it. Other times, after baking, it gets garnished with chopped scallions and cilantro. This is a gateway pizza. Once you make it, you'll find yourself experimenting. But do so judiciously. Again, too much moisture in your toppings and you get soup.

REFRIGERATOR PIZZA

This is a fun pizza. Why? Because it's a little bit like Christmas morning. You never know what you're going to get. The way I make this is I literally go through the fridge and see what I have that might make a good topping. The last Refrigerator Pizza we had included: andouille sausage, Black Forest ham, crimini mushrooms, sliced onion, sliced Fresno chili, and a fresh cilantro garnish. Another such pizza began that way, and has now become a favorite (and certainly one of the prettiest): Italian sausage, crimini mushrooms, roasted red pepper, red onion, and a basil chiffonade. It's an explosion of color on a pizza, and tastes better at least because it looks so good. Over the years, there have been several such efforts that have evolved into favorite combos. Just be imaginative and not lock yourself into any kind of rigid thinking about what's on a pizza, and maybe you, too can create your own equally beloved and belittled Hawaiian pizza.

WHAT ELSE CAN YOU DO?

Anything. You are now a budding Pizza Subversive. We're going to discuss that in the next chapter…

WHAT ELSE IS PIZZA?

That's up to you. You are now a budding Pizza Subversive. You have had a glimpse inside the oven, and it's just not as difficult or daunting as it may have seemed.

Are you feeling as if we've provided too few recipes?

That was not the goal of this book. We said that right at the beginning: This is not a cookbook. This shows you a system for making great pizza at home using the oven you already have.

YOU DON'T NEED RECIPES

I've said this to people who think I'm crazy. One woman I know said, "Yes, I do need recipes." I replied, "No you don't. Anyone can cook. You choose to have recipes. There's a difference." Now, she's confronted with a family of eaters who are scandalously picky and proud of it. For her, recipes might just be her way of throwing in the towel. Experimentation is not on the table, either metaphorically or literally. And that's sad.

Once you have the chemistry part of the pizza down (that would be the dough), and you understand the thermodynamics (what the oven does), you can experiment like crazy.

I've started keeping a pile of small dough balls in my fridge and freezer. They're about the size of a racquetball. They are specifically for experimentation. Just last weekend, I thought, "What about fontina and onion with prosciutto and arugula?" I did a quick search of the recipes available online just to see what the basics and commonalities were. And 90 minutes later, I had a 9-inch pizza on the table that was excellent—not because I loved it (I didn't) but my wife did (and that's key).

Now that you know the discipline of being a pizzamaker, you have a whole world of experimentation open to you and your pizza palate.

Or not. Maybe you want to stick with the basics. That's fine. You still get to make those pizzas the best they can be.

IS THE LIST OF COMBOS IN THE LAST CHAPTER TOO SHORT?

Yes. It is a list of classics that nods to the list of America's favorite pizza toppings. But you can put anything you want on a pizza. Got some leftover beef stew and American cheese? I'd be curious to see that pizza. I'd make sure the stew was thick enough. Maybe put it on the stove and add a little flour to give the gravy enough body to hold up as a pizza sauce. I have some green chili in the freezer that I've been thinking about trying as a pizza topping. There are just three limiting factors in all this:

1. Imagination
2. Physics
3. Prejudice

No, that last one is not a joke. It's kinda sad. Let's look a little deeper…

Imagination: You can dream up pizza ideas all day long if you want. It costs you nothing, and it will not end up as a pile of hot, wet garbage in the middle of your oven. It's only a brainstorm, not a real world kitchen incident.

Physics: This is how kitchen incidents happen. We're talking about the place where the rubber meets the road and the pizza meets the peel. You can dream all day long, but when it comes to physical implementation, no pizza dough like the one in this book is going to hold seven pounds of pulled pork and pequin peppers covered in Laughing Cow cheese.

Because of physics, restraint is your friend. Balance makes beauty. Too much of any good thing becomes a nightmare you need to repair using a shovel.

Prejudice: When it comes to inventing your own pizza, one of the worst phrases you can hear is, "That's not a pizza!" Worse is the uninformed, one-word commentary: "Disgusting!" Well, my friend, how do you know this measure of disgust you profess?

Yes, if you're allergic to shellfish, trying a shrimp and garlic pizza is stupid. To you, especially if you've had a near-death experience related to ingesting a food product, a gag reflex is understandable and possibly even a lifesaver from death by anaphylactic shock. Be disgusted!

That said, there is almost nobody with an allergy to cooked pineapple. The way many people know they hate pineapple on pizza is they won't try it.

How's that for a non-sequitur?

(Raw pineapple is a different story. A small percentage of individuals suffer from Oral Allergy Syndrome, a condition which is usually limited to raw fruits and vegetables.)

I have family members who hate the mere idea of sushi so they won't try it. That's unfortunate and illogical. But then again, man is not a logical animal. Logic happens in spite of the human penchant for emotional reaction. Still, as far as pizza goes, deciding what is and is not allowable based purely on ignorance is what prevents magic from happening. (There are pizzas I keep secret. Few people have had them. And they are glorious.)

That said, I have uninformed opinions. Gold leaf on pizza is stupid. There, I said it. And if I have to explain myself, you are clearly in the wrong book. Yet you somehow made it this far.

All this to say: Keep an open mind. Don't taste anything until you put it in your mouth. Yes, it might be a bad idea. Speaking of bad ideas, I know someone who says that, as a starving student cooking for himself, he forced himself to eat all his mistakes. Some years later, he said he wasn't sure that was a good idea. I concur— but I always at least taste my mistakes. Rarely is anything inedible. But don't torture yourself.

Thank you for making it through this book. I love pizza and I like sharing the joy. Thank you for joining me in pizza subversion. You now have the power to make pizza happen in a way that moves mountains, changes the course of mighty rivers, wins friends, influences people, and eventually makes some stranger say to you, "I've heard of you!"

Free the pizza!

SEND US YOUR PIZZAS!

Have you made a pizza of which you are particularly proud? Send us a photo! We'll put it on the Free The Pizza Wall of Fame along with other pizzas made by folks just like you.

Visit www.FreeThePizza.com, and use the form on the contact page.

APPENDIX

YOUR OVEN, YOUR BROILER, AND YOU...

The broiler in your oven is one of the best things that ever happened to homemade pizza. It helps you to mimic the high heat of a professional pizza oven in your modest consumer appliance. You heat the oven (and your baking stone or steel) for an hour at the highest temp, often 550 degrees.

Then, you flip the oven to broil on high, and slide your pizza into the oven.

However, different ovens have different parameters.

NO BROILER IN THE TOP OF THE OVEN

This is challenging. The good news: You do not need a broiler to make great pizza. And if you have a broiler in the bottom of your oven, you might want to avoid the broiler altogether. Just bake your pizza in the top of your oven at 550 degrees (or whatever the hottest setting is). It might take about 10 minutes. Maybe more. Maybe less. It will depend on the oven and the baking surface.

You'll want to rotate the pie 180 degrees at least once so that it bakes evenly. Just let it bake until the crust is browning nicely, remove it from the oven and serve to your astonished and appreciative guests.

So, no broiler? No problem.

Now, when it comes to using the bake/broil method, there are a few considerations.

THE ELECTRIC OVEN

If you have the most common kind of broiler, which is an electric oven with a broiler in the top of the oven, there is a simple procedure. It will also require some experimentation, as all ovens behave a little differently.

Place your baking surface in the electric oven at about 4 inches beneath the broiler element. (Sometimes, it has to be more. That's OK.) Set the oven to bake at the highest setting. Most ovens I've used go to 550. Some ovens top out at 525. I'm sure there are some that are lower. I've seen some that are higher.

Once the oven reaches temperature, allow it to continue heating for one hour. We have to make that thermal mass in your baking surface get hot hot hot and retain that heat for baking.

The common wisdom is that the broiler in an electric oven is set to turn off at 500 degrees. As a result, when heating your oven on bake to 550 degrees and switching to the broiler, the broiler will not come on immediately.

Accordingly, when you turn the oven to broil and slide in the pizza, you close the door just enough so that it's ajar at the top. The baking surface will stay hot, and the oven will vent enough heat so the broiler goes on. When the broiler turns red, go ahead and close the door all the way.

When you have a fully baked pizza and you've removed it from the oven, turn the oven back to the highest bake setting. Let it continue to heat the baking surface. (Of course, if you're not making any more pizzas, just turn it off.)

It is possible to worry about the oven door and the broiler. My experience has been that it's better to just pay attention without becoming obsessive. I've made five pizzas in a row in a marginal electric oven without paying too much attention to what the broiler is doing, and it works out OK.

The biggest challenge here is when making multiple pizzas. The baking surface is going to start cooling down. That's why I like to use the thickest baking steel possible. All that thermal mass retains the most heat under consistent use. The less mass you've got (or the more anemic your oven), the more you'll want to let it re-heat before baking the next pizza.

THE GAS OVEN

Gas broilers are different. In the main, my experience has been that the gas broiler goes on and stays on—unless you leave the door ajar. If the door isn't shut, the broiler doesn't go on. This is likely not the case with all gas ovens, just the ones I've used.

This means that you need to be more alert.

Place your baking surface in the oven at 6 inches below the broiler element. Set the oven to bake at the highest temperature setting. Most ovens I've used go to 550. Some ovens top out at 525. I'm sure there are some that are lower. I've seen some that are higher. (I used to have a 1950s vintage range that got up to 650 degrees.)

Once the oven reaches temperature, allow it to continue heating for one hour. We have to make that thermal mass in your baking surface get hot hot hot and retain that heat for baking.

When you're ready to bake your pizza, turn the oven from bake to high broil.

When you slide your pizza into the oven, close the door.

Be vigilant. The broiler in a gas oven seems to cook the pizza more quickly, and it isn't as even. Be prepared to rotate the pizza sooner than if you're using an electric oven.

When you have a fully baked pizza and you've removed it from the oven, turn the oven back to the highest bake setting. Let it continue to heat the baking surface. (Of course, if you're not making any more pizzas, just turn it off.)

THE BOTTOM BROILER CHALLENGE

We addressed this at the beginning of this section under "No Broiler In The Top Of The Oven." We're doing it again here to prevent any unfortunate situations.

If you have one of those gas ovens where the broiler is a shelf in the bottom of the oven, save yourself. Do not use it. There are various methods suggested by various sources. I've not had great luck with them. The pizza you produce isn't great. My steel doesn't heat as it should. Sometimes, the broiler is on a thermostat like an electric oven, so it goes off when you don't want it to. Working that close to the floor with a peel is dicey.

I once sent a pizza sliding into the very back of the broiler. It hit the back wall of the oven and curled under and around the end of the shelf like a taco shell, sending cheese and toppings everywhere. I was able to rescue and serve it, but it was not pretty. As mentioned at the top of this section, just bake the pizza up top, no broiler. It will take longer, but it will still be quite good.

PREPARING FOR SPONTANEOUS PIZZA NEEDS

Far better than having a frozen pizza in your freezer is having a freezer full of dough balls and sauce. For example, at 3pm, my wife says, "Do you mind if I go out with the girls tonight?"

I say, "Of course not."

That's because I know she doesn't want to eat a lot of pizza. But I do.

And in my freezer are a) portioned bags of pizza sauce, and b) several 6-ounce dough balls—perfect for making a pizza for one.

I slip into the freezer and pull out a dough ball and a portion of sauce. I set it in the warmest place in the kitchen, which happens to be the top of the fridge (unless the oven is on). It begins to thaw.

At 5pm, when my wife leaves, I turn on the oven to 550 degrees. The baking steel is already inside. I move the thawing dough ball over by the heating oven.

By the time the oven is ready to go, which is about 90 minutes later, the dough ball has thawed sufficiently. If I happen to be using a larger dough ball which isn't thawing as rapidly, I will flatten it somewhat to speed thawing.

Near the end of the oven's heating cycle, I grate the cheese that's in the fridge, acquire and prepare whatever toppings I've decided to use, and hey—pizza party for one.

It's easy to do, not a big production, it tastes far better than a frozen pizza, and there's a certain degree of satisfaction in the process.

TAKING YOUR SHOW ON THE ROAD

As mentioned elsewhere in this book, I've made pizza across this great land of ours. I've been known to show up at friends' homes to throw a pizza party using their kitchens. They love it. And I get the bonus of being able to make pizza without having to clean up after company. (I always clean up the kitchen after. That's a must. I always leave it as I found it or better.)

I don't recommend doing this until you're comfortable enough with making pizza that the idea of walking into a strange kitchen and making five pizzas doesn't seem daunting.

So, with all this gear, how do you move your pizza shop into the car and over to a friend's house?

THE CANVAS TOTE BAG IS YOUR FRIEND

I have two large canvas totes. One is for the steel exclusively. The other is for the trays, peels and giant cutting board I use as a work surface. I never assume anyone has a good enough cutting board. I have a friend with a gigantic kitchen whose biggest cutting board is the size of a paperback book. I need a big work surface, so I bring it.

COOLERS & CONTAINERS

We've spoken about *mis en place*. I bring it with me. I do all prep at home. Shredding cheese, cutting toppings, par-cooking the bacon, etc. Everything gets its own plastic container. Mostly, I use those so-called disposable plastic containers which I never dispose of. The smallest and near smallest ones are great for small quantities of chopped toppings. I use bigger snap-lid containers for grated cheese and sauce.

Yes, I always cook the sauce ahead of time, too. Everything is prepped before leaving the house. I want as little friction in the host home as possible. And if you're having to chop veggies and slice meats and cook sauce, it's inconvenient at best. It bites into socializing time. And it makes your job look hard, and you never want that to happen. Nobody should see you sweat.

After all toppings and other ingredients are prepped (don't forget the dust!), I transport them in a soft-sided cooler along with my pizza cutter. Usually, everything fits into a single, soft-sided 16-can cooler. Yes, it was designed for transporting 12-ounce cans. I like the size and the form factor.

NOTE: Always research your oven ahead of time. Know whether it is gas or electric, top broiler or bottom. If the latter, you'll need to forego broiling and just bake. And yes, all of these things could be figured out as soon as you arrive. But it's nice to have as much intel ahead of time as possible.

THE CHEAT SHEETS

These are the cheat sheets. They're printed here so you can refer to them. If you want to scan them with your phone or other scanner, go for it. Or, visit www. FreeThePizza.com/cheatsheets to find downloadable PDFs.

PIZZA DOUGH CHEAT SHEET

THE TOOLS

Mixing bowl (big enough for your head)

A similar bowl (you may clean the one above and use that)

Measuring cup(s)

Measuring spoons

Pastry or basting brush

OPTIONAL TOOLS

Bowl scraper

Bench scraper

INGREDIENTS

All Purpose Flour, Unbleached

Make sure it hasn't passed its best-by date. That can cause catastrophic failure.

Water

Tap water is fine unless your tap water tastes awful. Then, use bottled water.

Table Salt

Any salt is fine, though I like using stupidly expensive salt from Utah.

Instant Yeast

This is also known by two common brand names, among others: "Quick-Rise" (Fleischmann's) or "Rapid-Rise" (Red Star).

Olive Oil

Beware: there's a lot of counterfeit olive oil out there. Buy a good, reliable brand. (More about that problem on our blog.)

MAKING THE DOUGH

Measurements

5 cups unbleached all-purpose flour

2 teaspoons of table salt

1 teaspoon instant yeast
1 3/4 cups cool water

DIRECTIONS

1. Wash your hands.

2. In the large bowl, stir together the flour, salt and yeast. Combine well.

3. Add the water and stir with the spoon, then use your hands.

Mix it all until combined. Then, really get in there and knead.

Hold the bowl with one hand and knead with the other. Turn the bowl and fold the dough. Turn and fold. Turn and fold. Get aggressive. Use those muscles.

It will be sticky and gloppy. As you mix, and the water combines with the flour, the hydrating dough in the bowl will begin pulling the shaggy dough from your hand.

4. Keep kneading for about 5 minutes.

The dough should be a coarse-looking ball, sticky to the touch.

Not sticky? Add a tablespoon of water and knead some more.

Too sticky? Add a tablespoon of flour and knead some more.

You want a ball that looks rough and feels tacky.

5. Let the dough rest for five minutes.

The flour becomes further hydrated. Shouldn't you? Have a beverage.

6. After five minutes of rest, return to kneading.

Go for several minutes until the ball begins to appear smooth.

If it's easier to remove the dough ball from the bowl and knead it on a cutting board, go nuts.

Try pulling the side of the dough nearest you up and away from you, folding the dough over on itself. Then turn it 90 degrees and repeat.

In a perfect world, it will remain a little tacky.

Do you now have a slightly tacky, smooth-ish ball? Good.

7. Windowpane test.

Tear off a chunk of dough. Roll it into a ball and flatten it.

Try stretching it until it's thin and translucent. You should be able to see light through it. If so, this is great.

If the dough is not windowpaning, if it just tears, let it rest some more.

Then try it again.

If you want to feel like you're doing something, knead it a little more. Sometimes, you just have to walk away and let the dough sit.

Other times, it's close enough to a proper windowpane that you can move on. As the dough sits and proofs, the windowpane issue often resolves itself.

NOTE: I will often do a knead/rest session of four cycles before I'm satisfied with the windowpane. Don't get bummed out if it doesn't work the first time. You'll get there.

8. Get the second bowl.

Presumably, it's clean. Brush it with a light coating of olive oil.

9. Dust a clean work surface with flour.

Turn the dough out onto it. Flatten the dough a bit. It will get a little squarish.

10. Fold dough onto itself.

Grab each of the "corners," fold them over each other, gathering the dough together into a ball.

With the gathered side down, put the dough ball into the new, oiled bowl. Cover with plastic wrap.

11. After 20 minutes, repeat step #8.

Making sure there's a light dusting of flour on the board, turn the giant dough ball out onto the surface, flatten it again, fold over the four corners to make a new ball, and put it back in the bowl.

12. Repeat the above step again.

That means waiting twenty minutes, then flatten and fold again.

13. After the third time, cover the bowl with plastic wrap again.

Let it sit on the counter for an hour or so. Then, move it into the refrigerator.

24 HOURS LATER...

14. Bring the dough out of the fridge.

Turn the dough out of the bowl onto a lightly floured surface. Cut the dough into three, four or six chunks and form them into balls.

Three balls should yield three pizzas about 15-16 inches.

Four balls should yield four pizzas about 14 inches.

Six balls will yield six pizzas that are 10-12 inches.

FIRST TIMER TIP: Go with six balls. Smaller pizzas are easier to handle, at least psychologically. As you become more confident, you'll feel better about making larger pies. Even a 10-inch pizza feels like an accomplishment. When you get to 16 inches, you'll feel like a pro.

15. Bag the dough.

Brush each dough ball with a tiny bit of olive oil. Put each one into a quart-size, zippered plastic bag. Put all the dough back into the fridge. (If you don't plan to use it all in the next 24 to 48 hours, go ahead and freeze it. **IF YOU FREEZE THE DOUGH?** Be sure to move it from freezer to refrigerator 24 hours before you plan to use it.)

CHEESE CHEAT SHEET

INGREDIENTS

Mozzarella cheese, low-moisture, whole milk

Hard aged cheese, Parmigiano, Romano, Asiago, sharp Provolone, or something similar

NOTE: As discussed earlier in the book, do not buy pre-shredded cheeses. They are coated with anti-caking agents, and often don't melt well.

PREPARATION

Shred the mozzarella using the large holes on a box grater.

These are the holes that give you a cheese shred that's about 1/4-inch wide.

Shred the hard cheese using the small holes on the box grater.

Bear in mind, this is about fine shreds, not a finely grated dust. We're talking about the holes in the grater that are about 1/8-inch wide.

QUANTITIES

We're practicing balanced pizza. All quantities here are ultimately judged by how they appear on the unbaked pie. All measurements here are approximate.

Have enough mozzarella to provide coverage with sauce still visible. When you no longer see sauce, you're getting a little heavy on the cheese.

It's always better to have too much shredded cheese available than too little. You can always save the leftovers for the next pizzas.

NOTE: While we specify amounts, your mileage will vary. More important than measurements is how it looks. Can you see the sauce peeking through the cheese? Yes? Fantastic.

Mozzarella

For a 10-inch pizza, I use a modest fistful of mozzarella. By weight, this comes to about **3 ounces**. By volume, it's about **1/4-cup**, loosely packed.

For a **14-inch pizza**, I use a generous fistful of mozzarella, which comes to about **4 ounces**, around **1/3 cup**.

For a **16-inch pizza**, I use a generous fistful plus. It's about **5 ounces**, around a **1/2 cup**.

General note: I always figure that a 1-pound block of low-moisture mozzarella is going to be enough for three 16-inch pizzas.

Parmigiano Reggiano or other hard cheese

For a **10-inch pizza,** I use a very generous pinch. By volume, it's about **1 table-spoon**. Maybe more, depending on how much coverage I get.

For a **14-inch pizza**, I use two generous pinches, which is about **2 tablespoons**.

For a **16-inch pizza**, I use two generous pinches plus. It'll be **2-3 tablespoons**.

PIZZA SAUCE CHEAT SHEET

INGREDIENTS

28-ounce can of tomatoes, whole, diced or crushed

Salt (about 1/4 teaspoon)

Olive oil (about 1 tablespoon)

Onion powder (about 1 teaspoon)

Garlic powder (about 1/2 teaspoon)

Dried basil (about 1 teaspoon)

In this recipe, measurements are secondary. The key is not the science of measurement, but how it tastes. Is it bold and memorable in a good way? Add more spices if you feel you need it.

Put the tomatoes into a saucepan. Grind using an immersion blender, or smash them with a potato masher.

Put tomatoes over medium heat.

Add a glug of good olive oil. Maybe about a tablespoon-ish. Maybe two.

Add salt to taste. The flavor of the tomatoes should begin waking up, making you think, "Hey, I'd eat more of that."

Add onion powder, garlic powder and basil.

When the tomatoes begin bubbling, reduce heat to simmer. Let simmer long enough to reduce the tomatoes to a thick-ish consistency. It will still be loose, but not watery. Depending on your heat, this can take 20-30 minutes.

Taste again. Is it good? Does it make you excited? It's done. If it doesn't taste salty enough, add a dash of salt. If it needs more herbal pop, add some more basil.

When it's thick enough that it looks coarse and tastes good, your sauce is ready. If you'd consider sitting down with the entire pot and a spoon, you've got pizza sauce.

BAKING THE PIZZA CHEAT SHEET

PREPARING TO BAKE

Remove the dough from the fridge.

This is important. If the dough doesn't come to room temp, it won't stretch.

Set the oven rack.

Move it up into the top third of the oven.

If your oven is electric...

There should be about 4 inches between the shelf and the broiler element.

If your oven is gas...

There should be about 6 inches between the shelf and the broiler element.

If you have a bottom broiler...

Don't use it. Bake your pizza only. Just place the oven rack near the top of the oven.

Place your baking steel, cast-iron pizza pan, or previously seasoned stone on that top rack.

It needs to heat up from cold with the oven.

Set the oven at its highest setting for baking.

On most ovens, that will be 550. Some go to only 525.

When the oven reaches temperature (probably 20 to 30 minutes), set a timer for 60 minutes.

You need to heat the baking surface for an hour in order for that thermal mass to fully heat up so it can make the pizza dough "pop."

STRETCHING THE DOUGH

We're assuming you're working with 6-ounce dough balls.

That yields a pizza about 10-12 inches.

Have your peel ready.

Dust the surface with semolina or cornmeal.

Dust your work surface with flour.

It requires enough flour that the dough doesn't stick to the surface and is easily workable.

Remove the dough ball from the bag.

Depending on how much the dough ball has risen, this might require slitting the bag with a sharp knife.

Place the dough ball on the floured work surface and flatten it with both hands.

While doing so, keep it round.

Rotating the dough, stretch it outward and continue flattening.

Keep going until it's about half an inch thick.

Using your fingers, dimple the dough all the way around, about half an inch inside the edge.

It's almost as if we're drawing a dotted line around the inner edge of the pizza.

Using both hands, stretch the dough out some more.

You want it to get wide enough that you can pick it up with both hands and get underneath it with your knuckles.

Make two fists and get your knuckles underneath the edge of the disc.

Stretch it with your knuckles, then rotate and stretch, rotate and stretch, until it's getting thin enough at the center that you're concerned.

Grab the very edge of the dough with both hands like a steering wheel.

Stretch the outer edge. Feel free to let gravity help you with this.

Stretch the edge of the dough until you've got a disc that's about 12 inches in diameter.

It might be smaller. It might be larger. But it will be about a foot across. It should be roundish.

Place the stretched pizza dough on the dusted peel.

If it's not round, rearrange the dough until it is.

Just arrange it gently, pulling or pushing the edges until it's round enough that you feel like you've accomplished something.

Pick up the peel and give it a little horizontal shake.

Is the dough sliding on the surface of the peel? Fantastic.

You have several minutes to put toppings on the pizza before it sticks to the peel.

TOPPING THE PIZZA

Scoop up some sauce with a big spoon or ladle, and start at the center of the dough.

Spread a thin layer of sauce around the pizza. Spread it as evenly as possible. You want to still see dough through the sauce.

Spread the sauce out to the edges.

Leave just enough dough un-sauced for the *cornicione* (or "the handle," as many Americans like to call it).

Sprinkle the mozzarella on top.

You want consistent coverage, and still have a fair amount of red sauce peeking through.

Once the mozzarella is spread, take a generous pinch of shredded hard cheese.

Hold your hand about two feet above the pizza and sprinkle it around. Do this a second time.

You now have a pizza that is ready to bake.

Pick up the peel with your pizza on it. Give it another little shake to be sure the pizza is still sliding.

Is the pizza NOT sliding?

Hold the peel up near your face. Lightly pinch the dough nearest you and lift it. Blow a little puff of air under the pizza. The whole pizza should puff up and settle back. Try giving the peel another little, horizontal shake. Does it slide now? If not, try puffing again.

Prepare to launch the pizza.

Go to the oven. Put the peel inside the oven at a slight angle. The tip of the peel should be near the back of the baking surface.

Give the peel a little jerk back towards you and slide it out, all in one motion.

The pizza should slide off the peel and onto the baking surface.

Close the oven door.

Turn the oven's temperature control to HIGH BROIL.

Set your timer for three minutes.

If your oven is electric, leave the oven door ajar until the broiler goes on.

Once the broiler is on, shut the door.

At three minutes, open the oven door.

If you're using two peels, now's the time to use the metal one.

Slip your peel under the pizza and slide it out.

Using your fingers but without burning yourself, gingerly rotate the pizza 180 degrees, and slide it back into the oven.

Close the oven door, and set the timer for three more minutes.

NOTE: If you're not using the broiler, you'll probably be going for an additional 3-minute cycle.

Peek at the pizza about every minute or so.

You may need to remove it before the three minutes are up. Or, it may need a little longer. If it's browning unevenly, you might want to rotate it again.

Is there a little char on it, with little black bubbles appearing around the edge of the crust?

That's good. Char is flavor.

If the pizza needs an extra minute or two to get to the char and bubble stage, that's fine.

Retrieve the pizza.

Slide the peel beneath it and pull it out of the oven.

Place it on a cutting board or a pizza tray.

Let it rest for a moment, so it begins to set.

Using your pizza cutter (or a chef's knife), cut the pizza.

Four, six or 8 slices will do.

Serve.

Are you going to bake another pizza? Switch the oven from BROIL back to BAKE at 550.

Let the baking surface heat back up while you enjoy your pizza.

ACKNOWLEDGMENTS

A special thanks goes out to everyone who helped make all this pizza possible. First of all, Chef John Courtney who took the plunge despite never having written a foreword before. To Barbara Grassey, who remains a timely and unimpeded editor despite now living on the siesta clock in a western European beach location. Thank goodness you can take the woman out of New England, but you can't take New England out of the woman. Thanks to everyone across the nation who has opened their kitchens to partake in the endless shower of pizza parties via the Free The Pizza Road Show, including Jeff & Jackie, Beth & Bill, George & Lori, Julie & Ted, Eric & Jodie, Charlie & Melba, Matt & Amy, and John & Paige. Plus, a special shout out to John & Deb, who've opened their kitchen repeatedly and even put in their own pizza baking hardware to develop an ongoing pizza delivery program inside their own home. And finally, to The Fabulous Honey Parker who always manages to turn a blind eye to her low-carb diet anytime a fresh pizza pops from the oven. This love apple pie is for you.

And, of course, a doff of the old pizza hat to you, dear reader, without whom this meager effort would be totally pointless.

Remember to show us your pizzas at www.FreeThePizza.com/contact

ABOUT THE AUTHOR

Blaine Parker is on a mission. For over 20 years, he's been obsessed with the critical, crowd-pleasing craft of making pizza at home. As founder of Free The Pizza Dot Com, he's dedicated to saving the casual cook from the injury, insult and sabotage of the internet's wildly popular "quick pizza" advice. Since 2003, he's been working with conventional home ovens from Los Angeles to New Jersey, from Utah to Mississippi. He has also owned dedicated pizza ovens, from a cute little outdoor oven to a beastly, 1,200-pound, wood-fired brute living in his own kitchen. A rogue pizzaiolo by night, Blaine Parker maintains the daytime façade of a mild-mannered marketing writer and voiceover performer. He has been well paid for performances for several big international pizza chains. Blaine's wife, The Fabulous Honey Parker, likes to say that he has the voice of a much taller man.

John Courtney (Foreword) is a Food Network Chopped Champion, has been Chef de Cuisine at the Cosmopolitan of Las Vegas, and served as Culinary Director at Simon Hospitality Group. He and his wife Paige have been called a "Culinary Power Couple" by the Las Vegas *Review Journal*. John cut his culinary teeth in France with a trial by fire at a series of Michelin restaurants. He and Paige currently own and run two Park City, Utah establishments, Chop Shop Park City and Fish Market Park City. John is most recognized for his monster sideburns, which look like they might be very hungry.